I0809924

BAUKUNST

BOZAR – CENTRE FOR FINE ARTS, BRUSSELS
A+ ARCHITECTURE IN BELGIUM
KOENIG BOOKS

Brussels, Belgium

Brussels, Belgium

Zürich, Switzerland

Lausanne, Switzerland

Spa, Belgium

Tongre-Notre-Dame, Belgium

Geneva, Switzerland

Geneva, Switzerland

Geneva, Switzerland

The early Proterozoic world would have looked largely flat and damp, an alien yet familiar landscape, with volcanos smoking in the background and shallow, brilliantly colored pools abounding and mysterious greenish and brownish patches of scum floating on the waters, stuck to the banks of rivers, tinting the damp soils like fine molds. A ruddy sheen would coat the stench-filled waters.

All beings in this bygone biosphere were prokaryotic– that is, they all lacked nuclei. Their genes were not packed into chromosomes wrapped by a nuclear membrane. They had evolved and distributed probably all the major metabolic and enzymatic systems.

With their minimal number of genes leaving them deficient in metabolic abilities, these organisms lived and still live necessarily in communities. They never function as single individuals in nature. Instead, in any given ecological niche, populations of several kinds live together, responding to and reforming the environment, aiding each other with complementary enzymes. The various kinds of organisms in the community, each present in enormous numbers of copies, coordinate the release of their enzymes according to the stages in a task. Their life cycles interlock, the waste products of one kind becoming the food sources of the next. Intricately meshed in this way, bacteria occupy and drastically alter their environments. In huge and changing numbers, they perform tasks of which individually they are incapable.

With other strains of population always living nearby, ready to contribute useful genes or metabolic products, and to reproduce under favorable conditions, the community's overall efficiency is continuously modulated.

Ordinary hazards of the environment-temperature variations, the quality and quantity of sunlight, the concentration of salts in the water, –all acted to diversify the populations in different places. In the face of starvation, there began to accumulate in the planetary patina a variety of successful new organisms with new semes, new metabolic pathways by which food and energy could be extracted from various raw materials.

By cycling gases and soluble compounds through atmosphere and water, these colonies formed cooperative dwellings, visible as tacky scums and purple and sienna patches, and strange, multilevel pastures. Generation after generation the topmost layers died from radiation exposure, but their remains shielded the lower layers, which accumulated sand and sediment to form a sort of living rug. Microbial mats and muds dominated the low-lying watery Archean landscape.

Shrunk to microscopic perspective, a fantastic landscape of bobbing purple, aquamarine, red, and yellow spheres would come into view. Inside the violet spheres of *Thiocapsa*, suspended yellow globules of sulfur would emit bubbles of skunky gas. Colonies of ensheathed viscous organisms would stretch to the horizon. With one of the microbial layer stuck to the rocks, the other end would crack and begin to penetrate the rock itself. Long skinny filaments would leave the pack of their brethren, gliding by slowly, searching for a better place in the sun. Multicellular filaments and tacky, textile-like crowds of cells would wave with the currents, coating pebbles with brilliant shades of red, pink, yellow, and green.

Showers of spores, blown by breezes, would splash and crash against the vast frontier of low-lying muds and waters.

Lynn Margulis and Dorion Sagan, *Microcosmos Four Billion Years of Microbial Evolution* [1986], Berkeley and Los Angeles, University of California Press, 1997. Selected extracts by Adrien Verschuere, revised by Dorion Sagan.

EDF R&D
30

le Cubotron

3
126
6
1211
1212

12.00

Besides the raw bodies that nature presents to our observations, besides the living organized bodies that grow and, growing still, reproduce themselves through their own organization, there is a vast group of organized bodies, singular through their number, the mode of creation, the development and variety of individuals that it includes, remarkable for the services that each of them provides.

These organized bodies can be considered as forming, in the whole of nature, a kind of reign similar – by its richness, its variety, the singularities of its prodigious development and the vagueness of its contours – to the other reigns imagined until now. Their study therefore poses the same problems and involves the same disciplines as the study of the other beings that the other realms offer to our observations.

If these organized bodies differ from the raw bodies to be found in nature, they differ otherwise, but they also differ from the living organized bodies. Like them, they present singular properties resulting from the isolation of their functions in differentiated organs; like them, they evolve, their growing perfection unfolding in the direction of always more developed organic specialization; like them, they are likely to be studied for the mechanical and physical phenomena of which they are the seat.

If, in the vast group of these bodies, I compare several lineages among themselves; if, in some lineages, I compare among them the bodies whose organization is more composed, I am apparently justified in seeing only the differences, in losing sight of the common characteristics and in considering as isolated the groups or individuals on whom my investigations are carried out. However, a more sustained observation makes it possible to distinguish in all these bodies characteristics that they have in common, which belong only to them, which are essential to them, and whose consideration justifies the isolation of the whole they form in the broader group of the bodies of nature.

We could likewise distinguish the organized bodies from the many products of our activity and the many organizations that we meet in our societies. If, for instance, we consider the various forms of social organization that govern our relationships, that regulate their way of life; if we consider the many products that result from a technical activity, we will find that between them and the bodies that occupy us, there is this difference that some have, and not others, an organized plastic form that gives them the singular properties that are to be observed there.

By observing slow and almost insensitive modifications, we can start from the raw bodies of nature or from the materials resulting from our creative activity to find first our primitive machines, then the more composite devices that follow them. We can imagine the constructed organized bodies as forming, as a whole, a distinguished mass, in the whole of the bodies of nature, by general differentiated characters, common to all the individuals that constitute it and belonging essentially only to these individuals. Not that such a mass exists in reality, since its contours are lost and merge, by insensitive gradations, in the formidable organization of the environment. It results only from a classification process, filling in the gaps in our intelligence that do not allow us to grasp, at a single glance, all the facts, causes and laws of the world in which we live. Since we can only achieve fragmented knowledge, this mass that our intelligence distinguishes even though its contours are elusive, it is convenient and effective for us to study it as if its existence were real.

Jacques Lafitte, *Réflexions sur la science des machines* [1932], Paris, Librairie Philosophique J. Vrin [coll. Varia], 1972.
© Librairie Philosophique J. Vrin.
Translated by Patrick Lennon. Extracts selected by Adrien Verschuere.

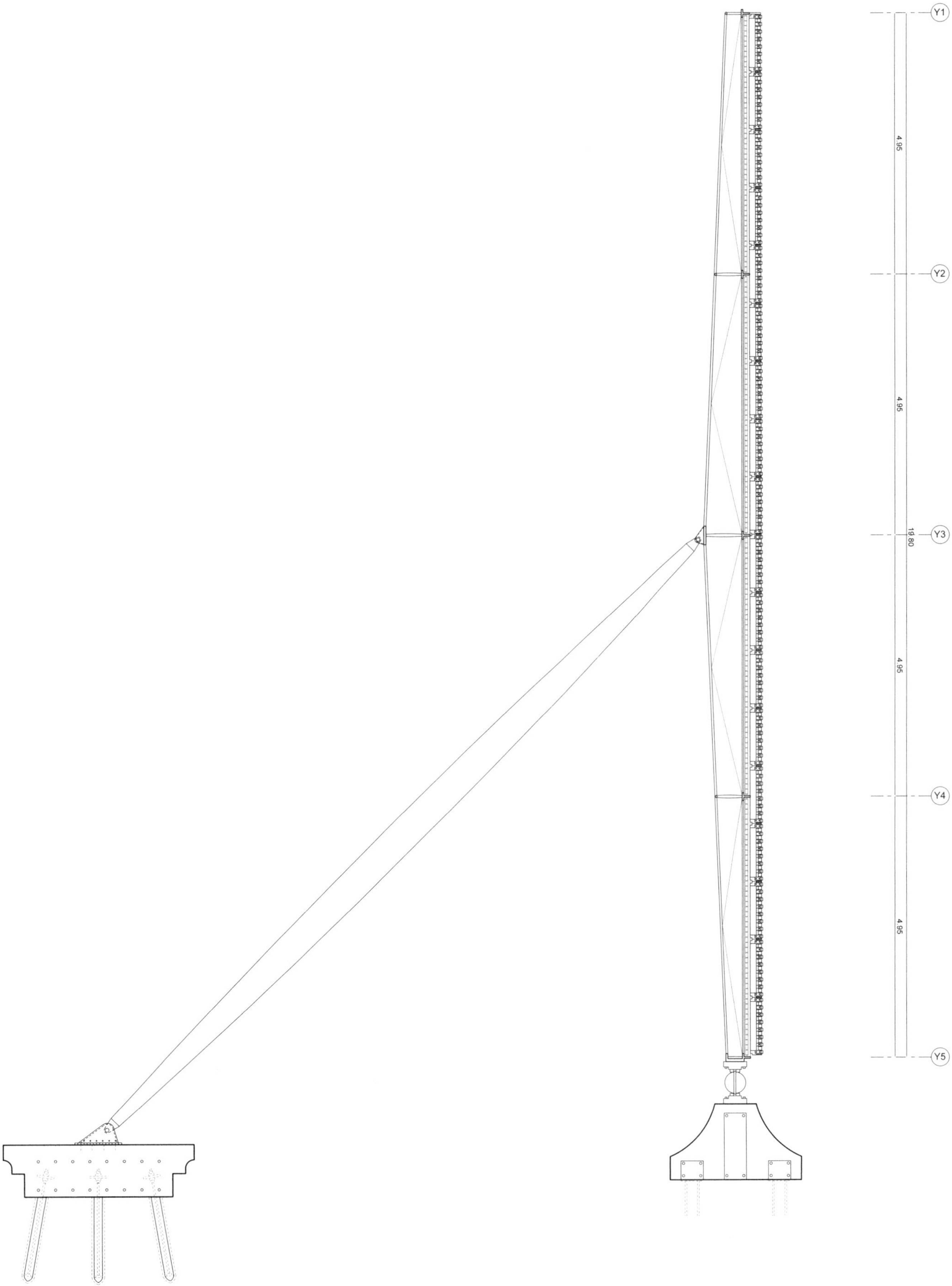

NMBS, Power station

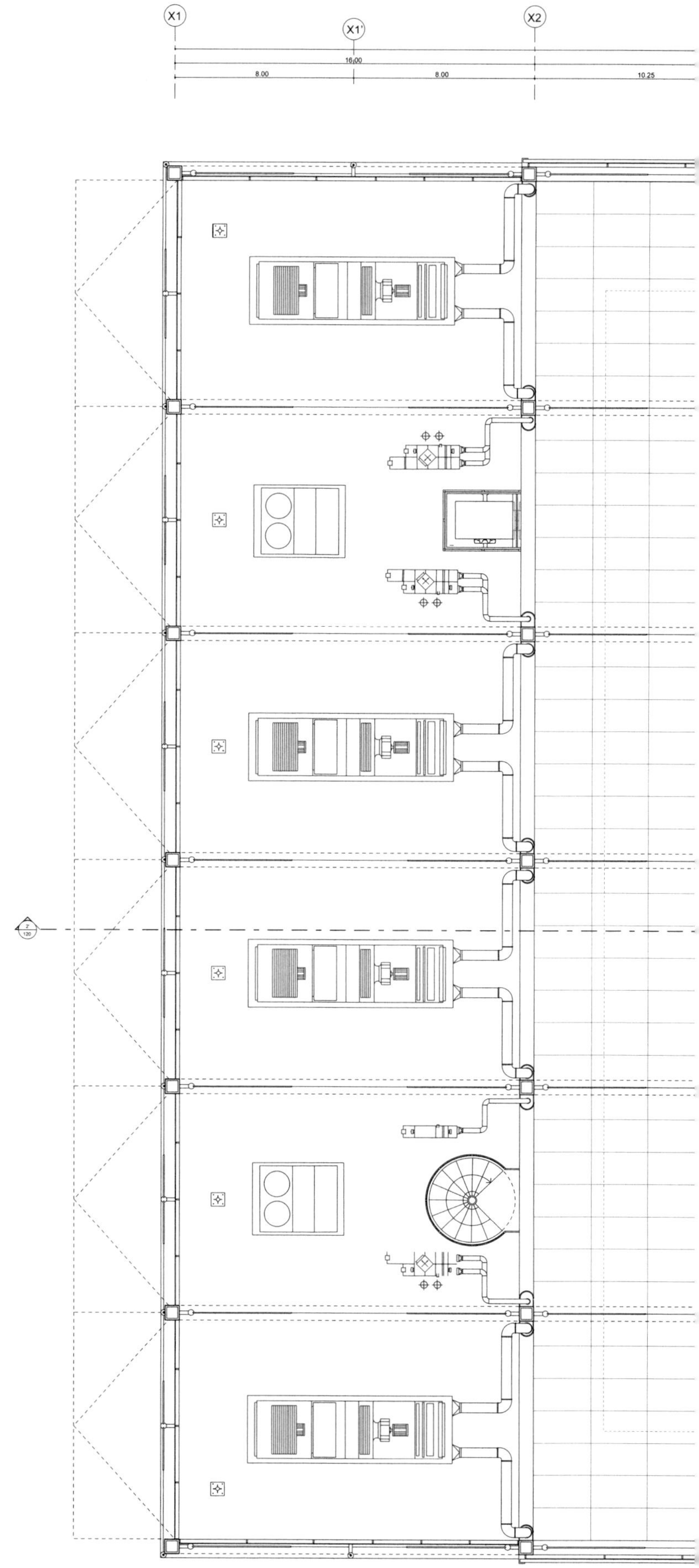
X1
X1'
X2
16.00
8.00
8.00
10.25

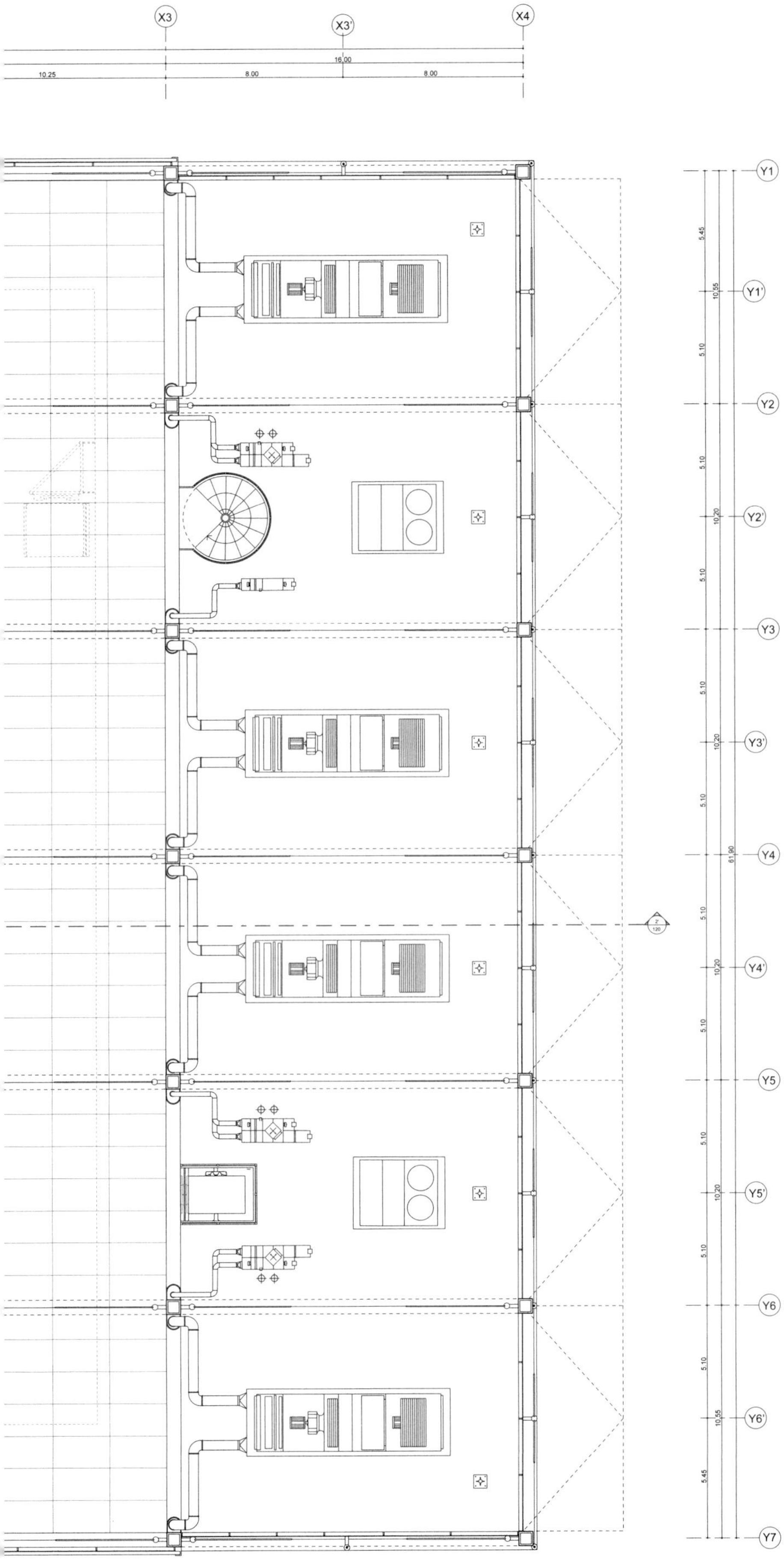
X3
X3'
X4
16.00
10.25
8.00
8.00
Y1
Y1'
Y2
Y2'
Y3
Y3'
Y4
Y4'
Y5
Y5'
Y6
Y6'
Y7
5.45
10.55
5.10
10.20
61.90

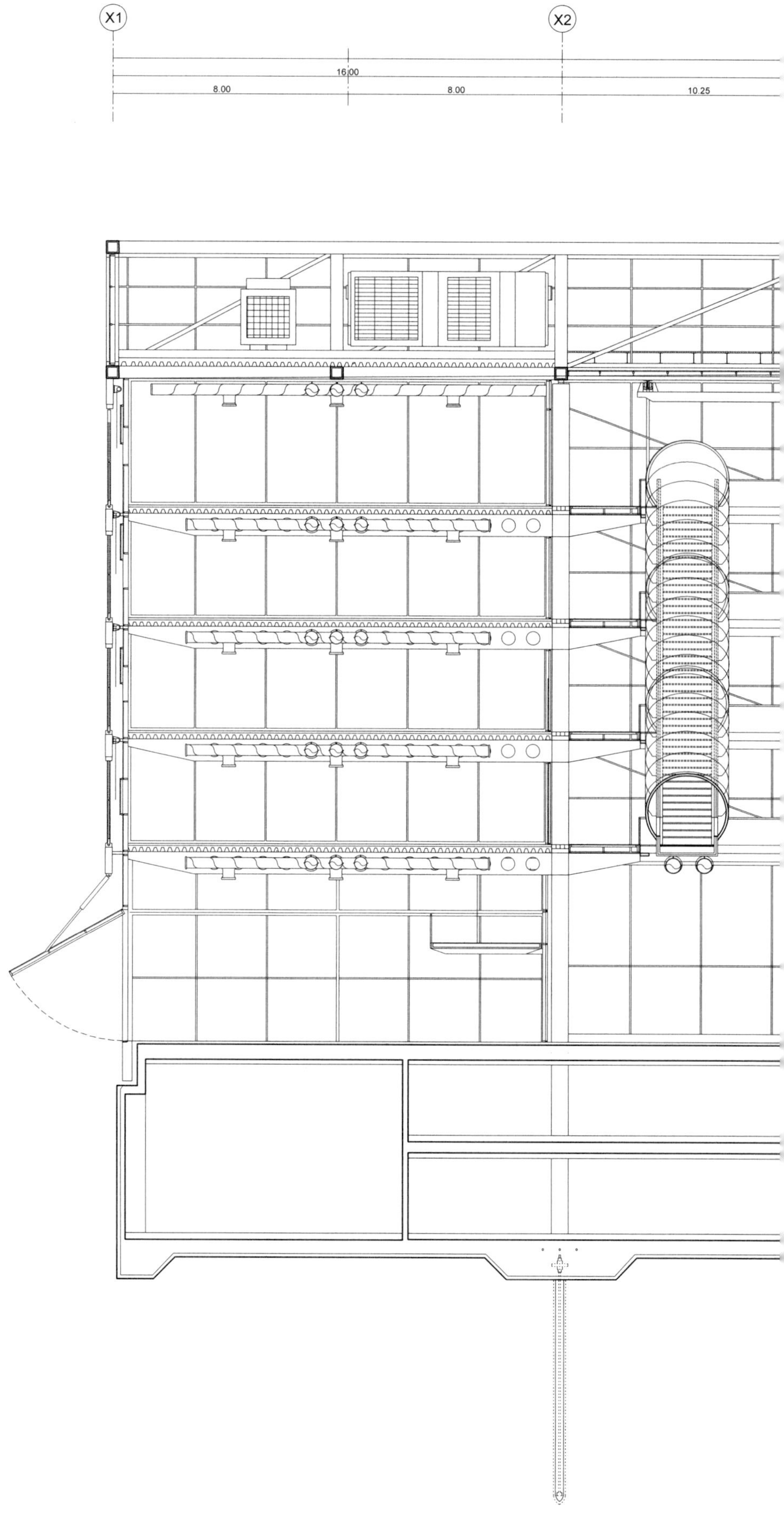
X1
X2
16.00
8.00
8.00
10.25

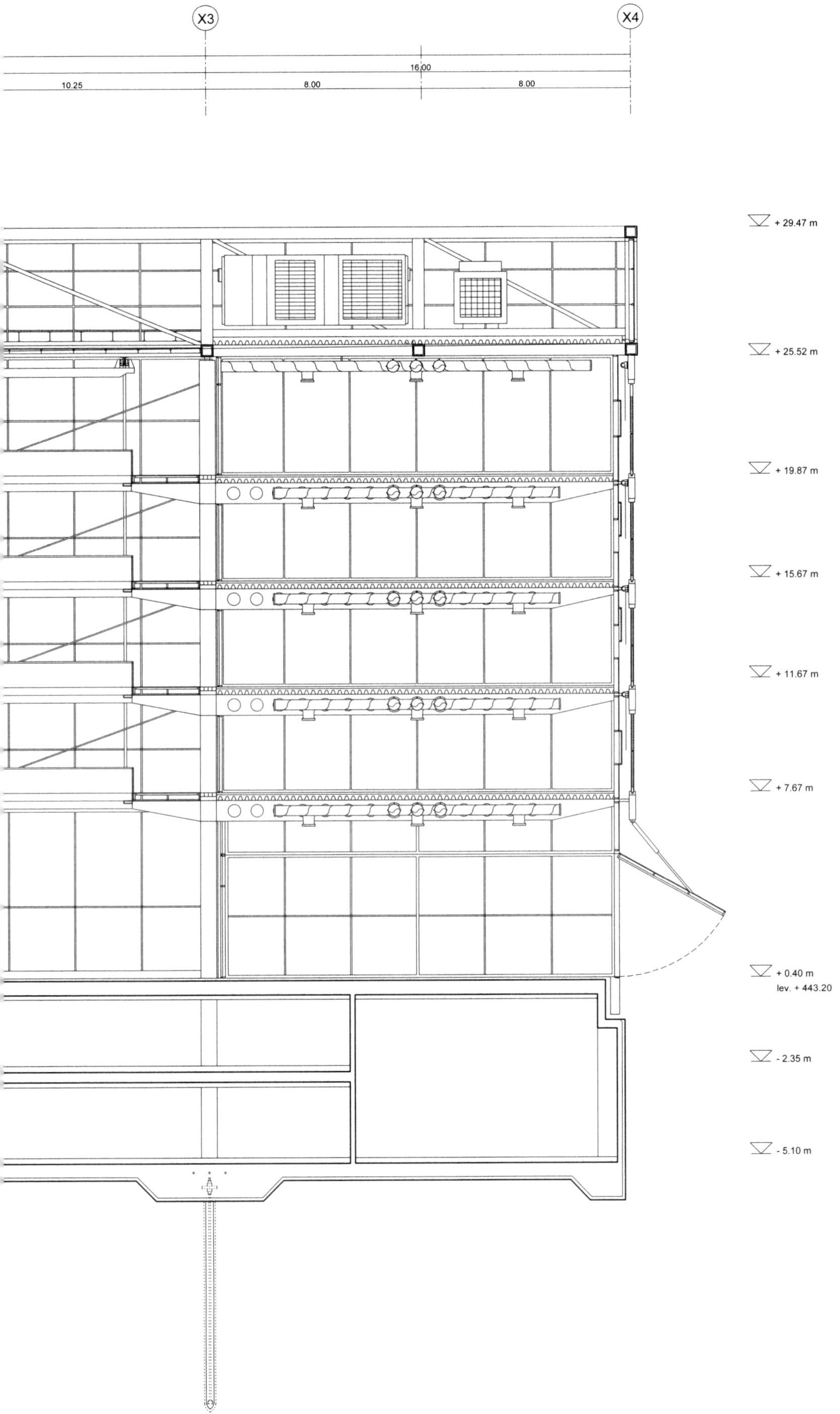
X3
X4
16.00
10.25
8.00
8.00
+ 29.47 m
+ 25.52 m
+ 19.87 m
+ 15.67 m
+ 11.67 m
+ 7.67 m
+ 0.40 m
lev. + 443.20
- 2.35 m
- 5.10 m

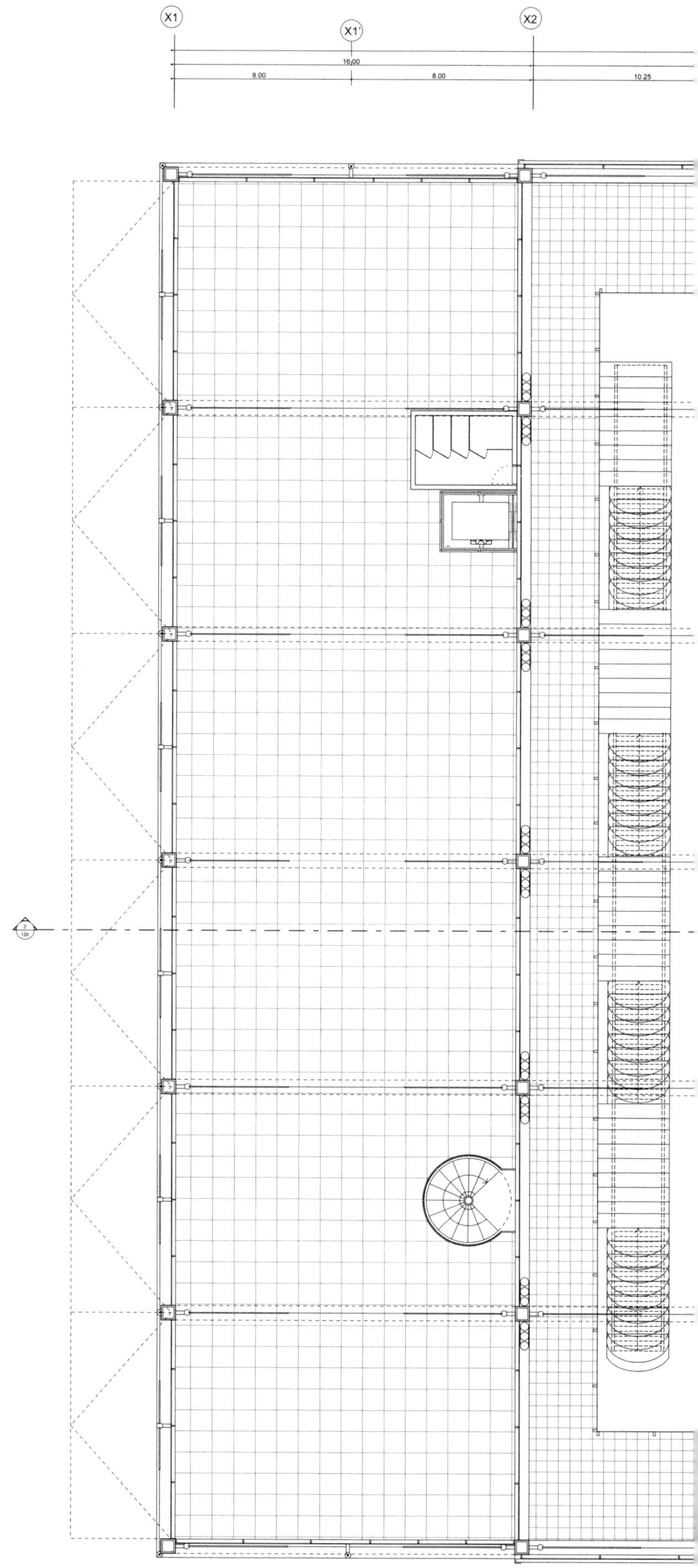
X1
X1'
X2
16.00
8.00
8.00
10.25

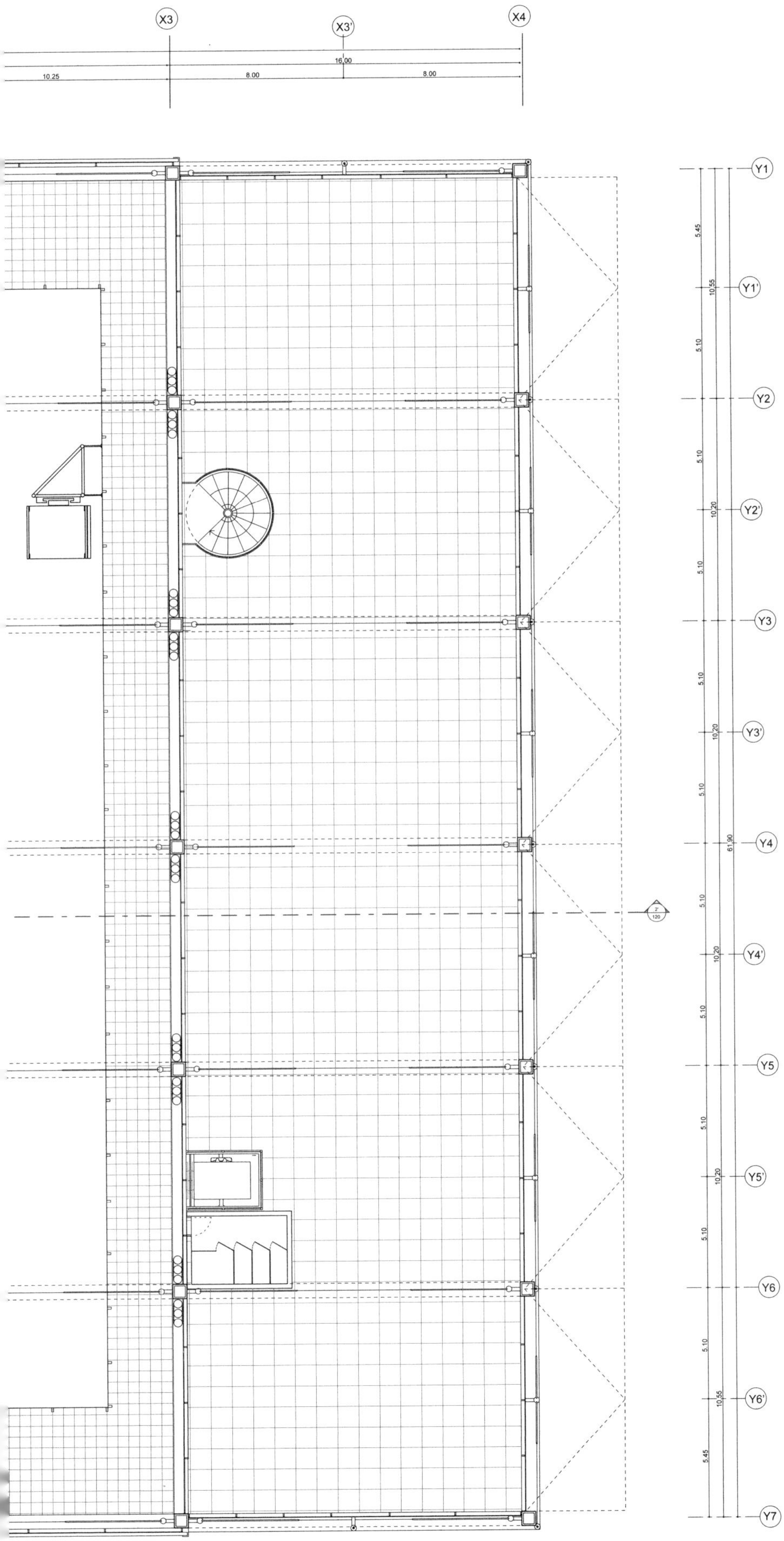
X3
X3'
X4
16.00
10.25
8.00
8.00
Y1
Y1'
Y2
Y2'
Y3
Y3'
Y4
Y4'
Y5
Y5'
Y6
Y6'
Y7
5.45
10.55
5.10
10.20
61.90

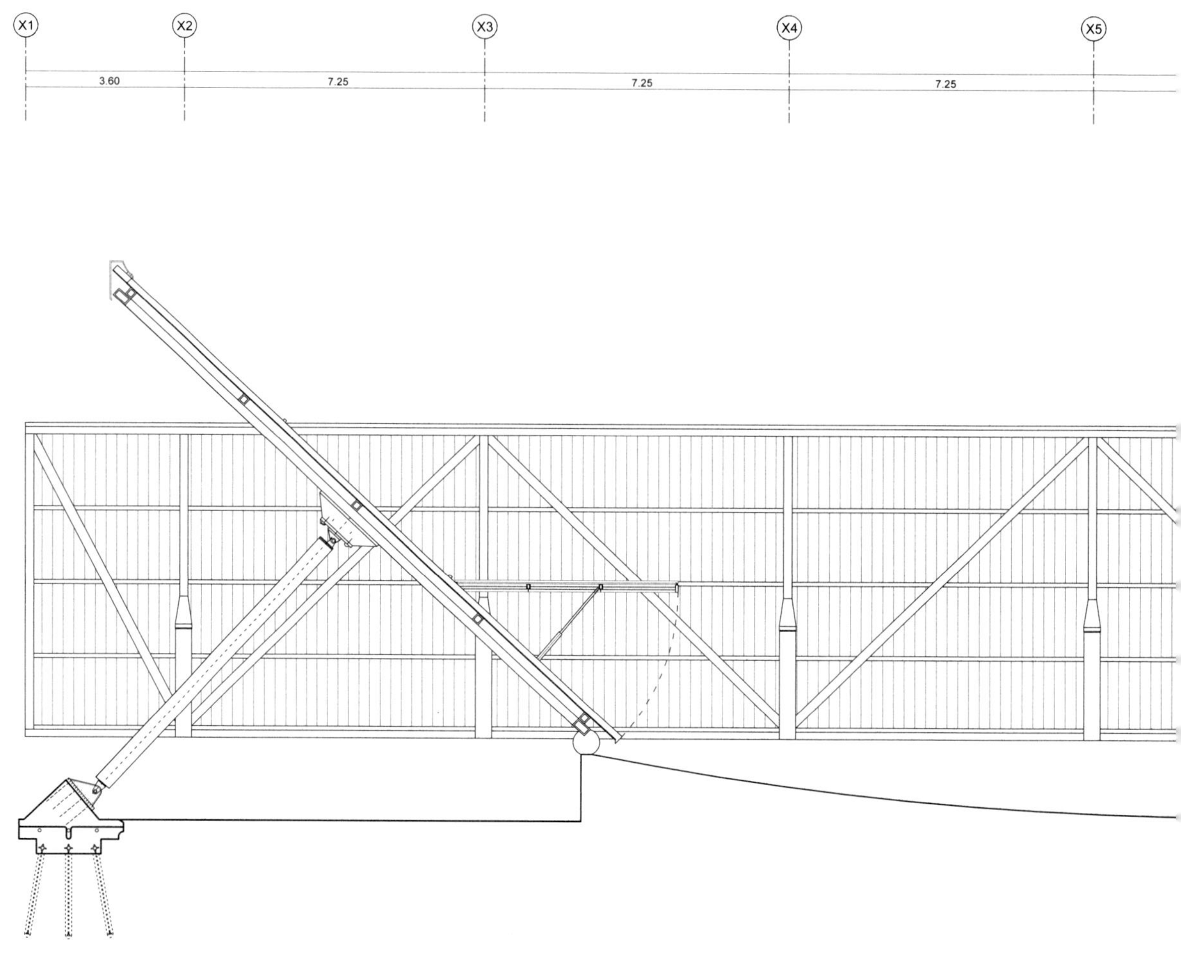
X1
X2
X3
X4
X5
3.60
7.25
7.25
7.25

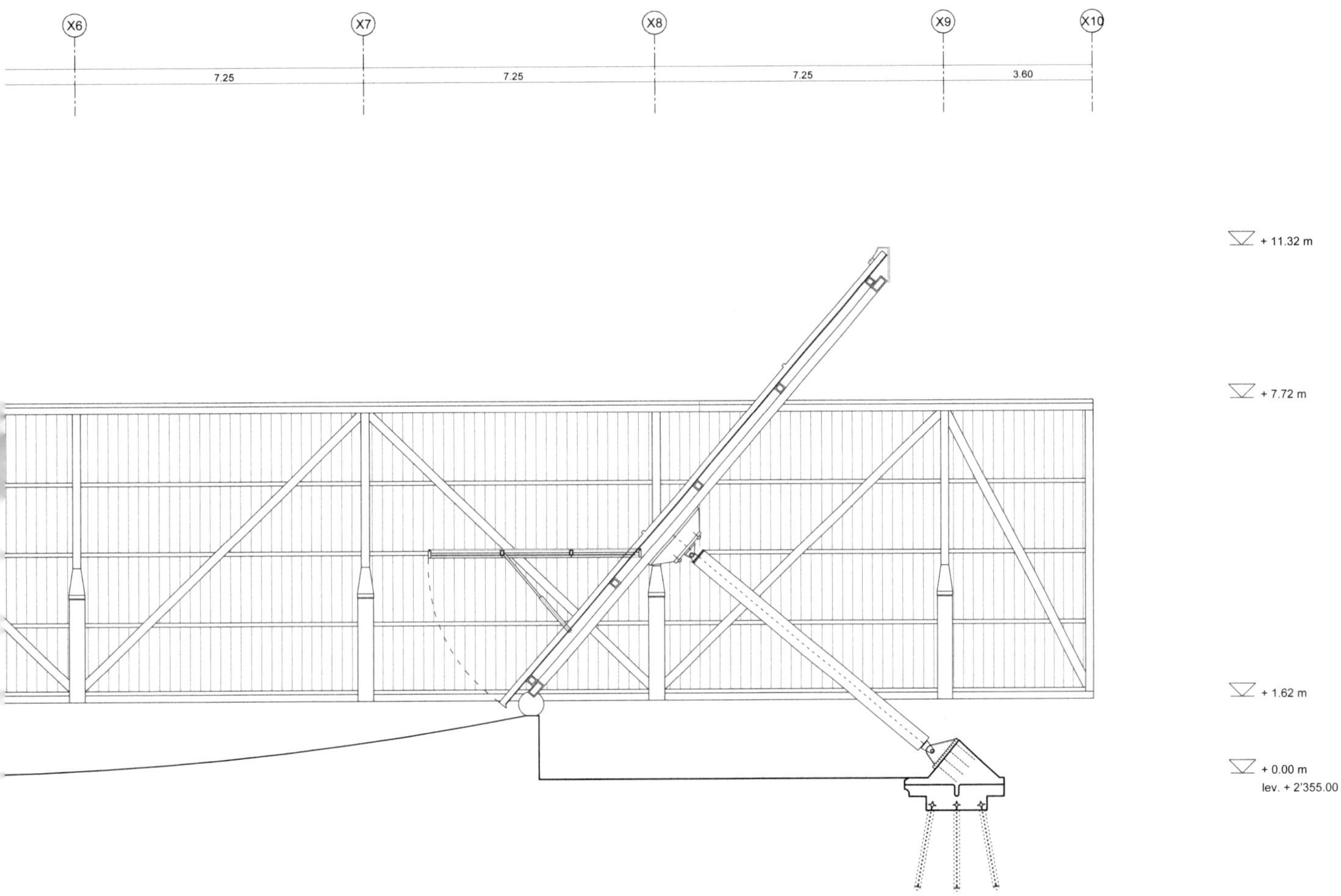

TORHAYLOCH HILL, Swiss embassy

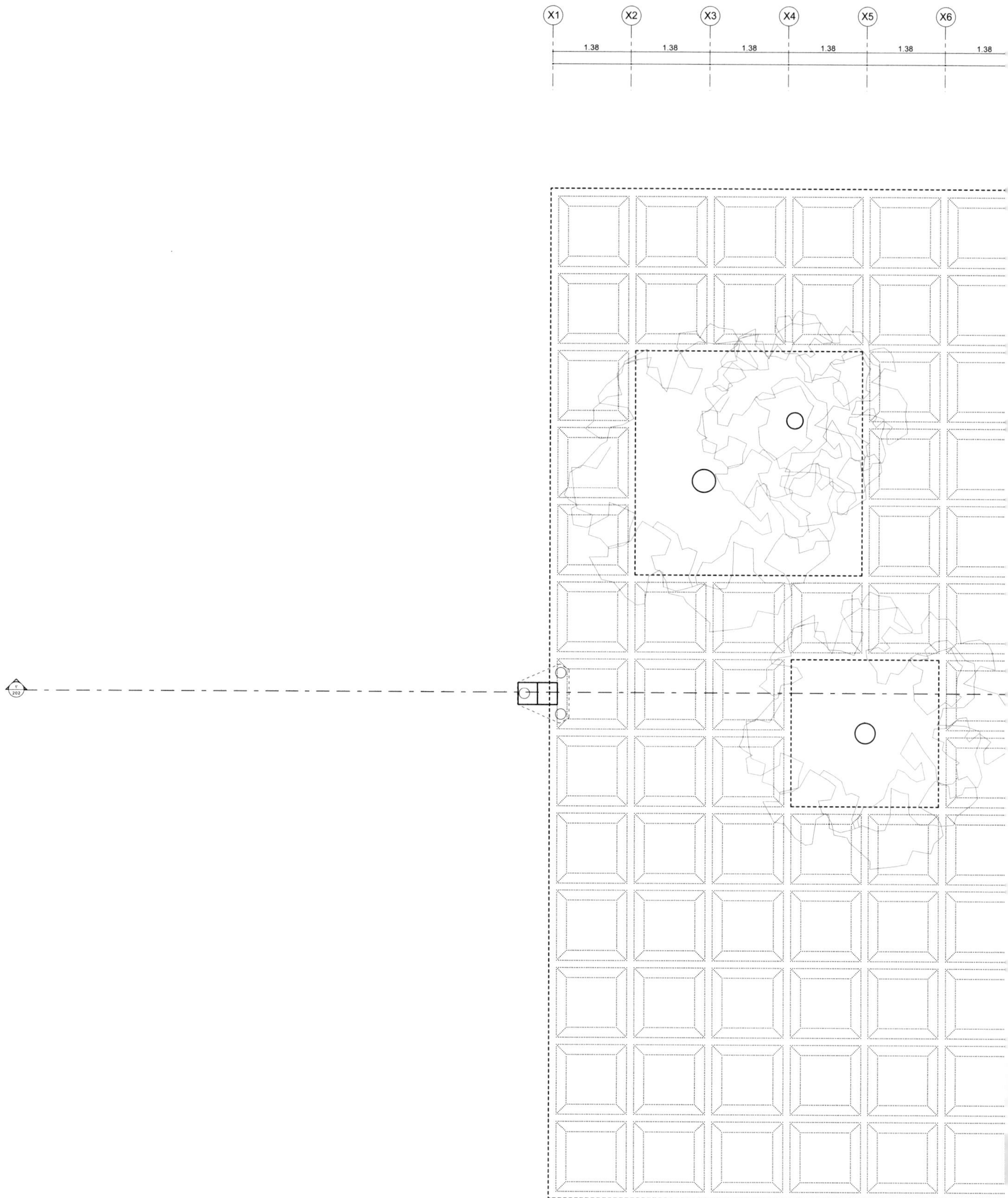
X1
X2
X3
X4
X5
X6
1.38
1.38
1.38
1.38
1.38
1.38
202

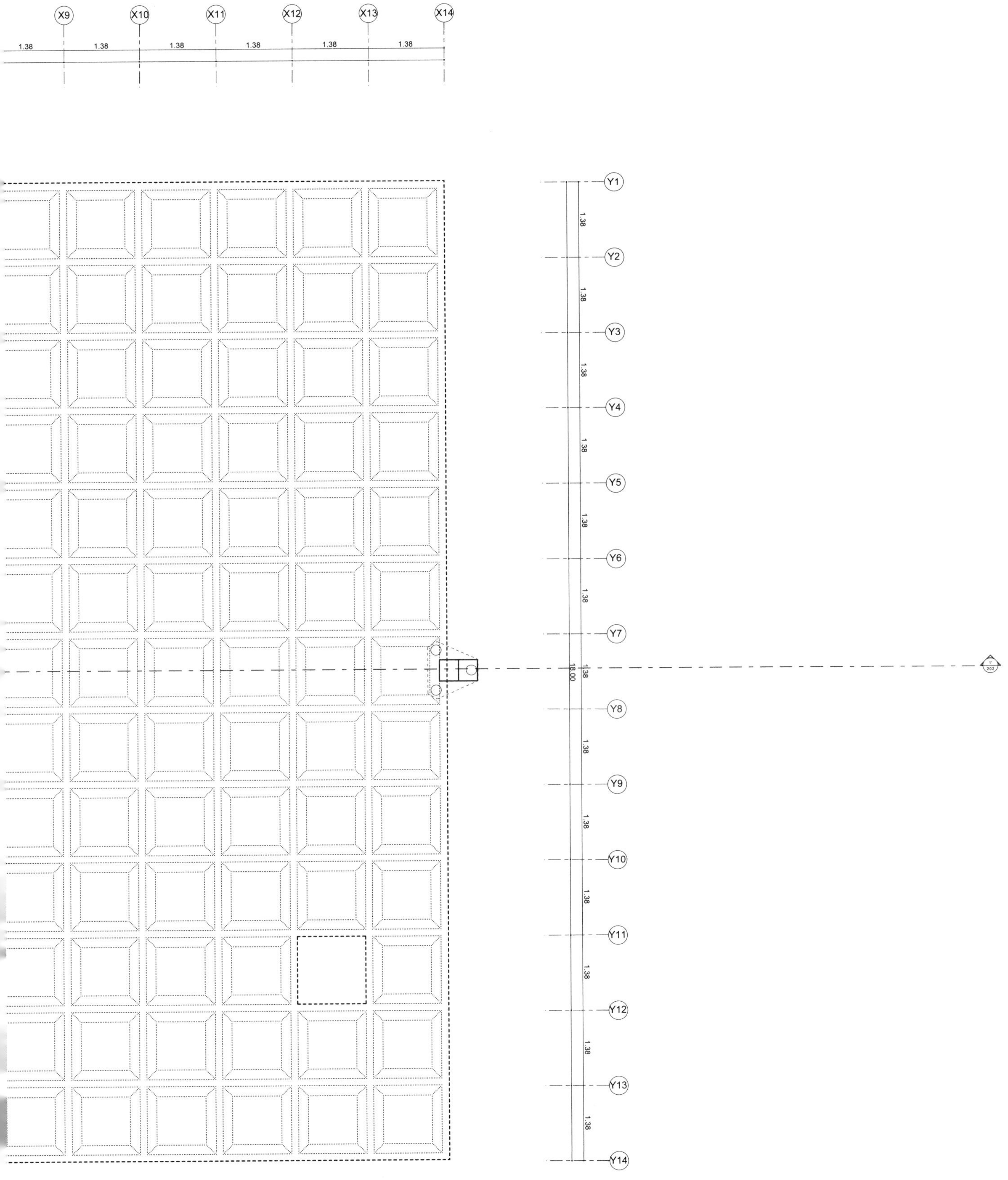
X9
X10
X11
X12
X13
X14
1.38
Y1
Y2
Y3
Y4
Y5
Y6
Y7
Y8
Y9
Y10
Y11
Y12
Y13
Y14
18.00
202

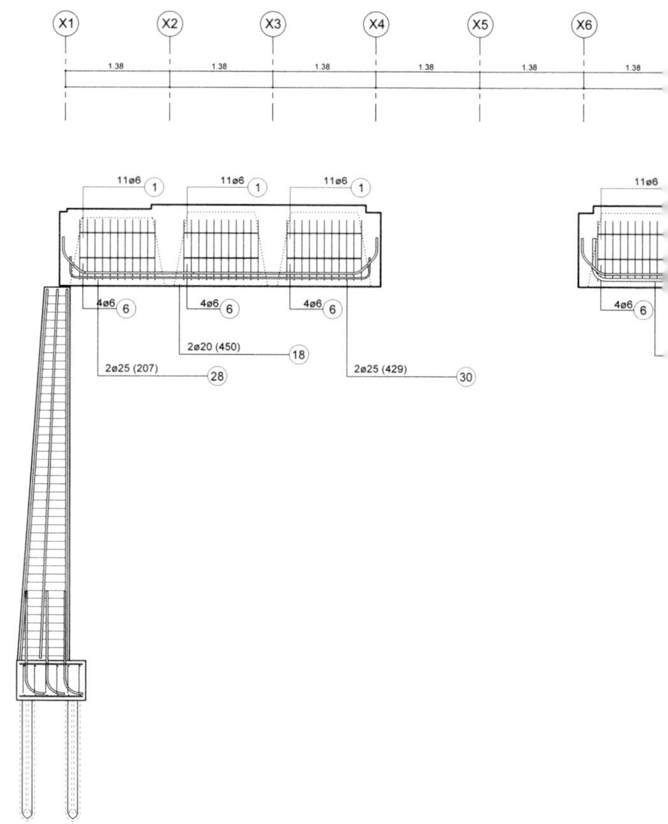
X1
X2
X3
X4
X5
X6
1.38
1.38
1.38
1.38
1.38
1.38
11ø6 1
11ø6 1
11ø6 1
11ø6
4ø6 6
4ø6 6
4ø6 6
4ø6 6
2ø20 (450) 18
2ø25 (207) 28
2ø25 (429) 30

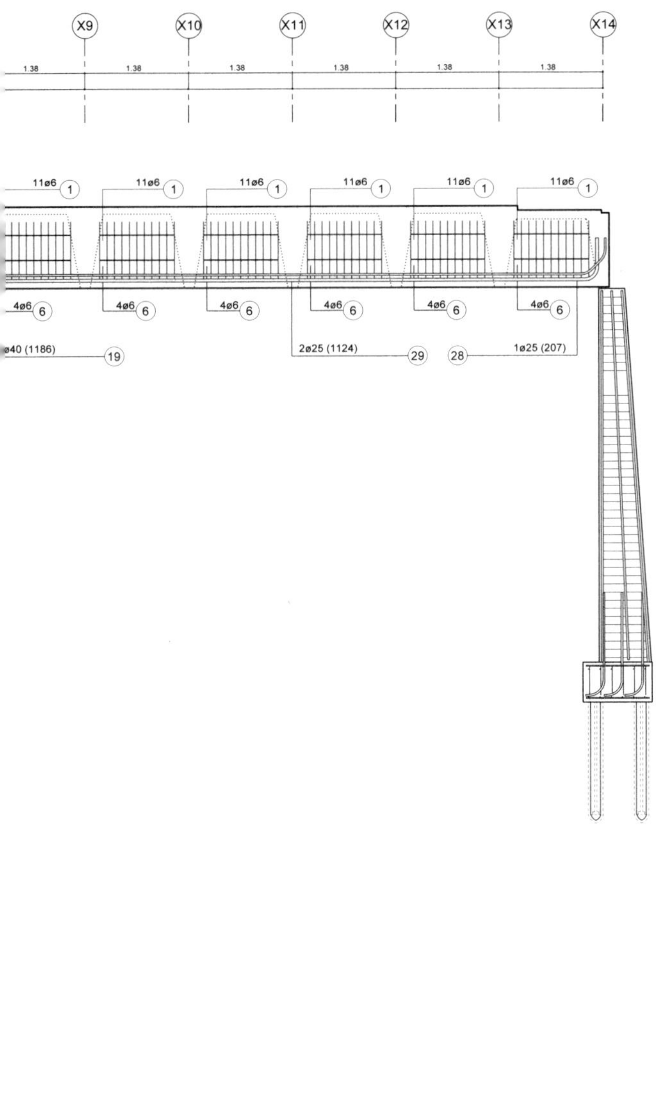

QUATRE-VENTS, Pocket park and polyvalent hall

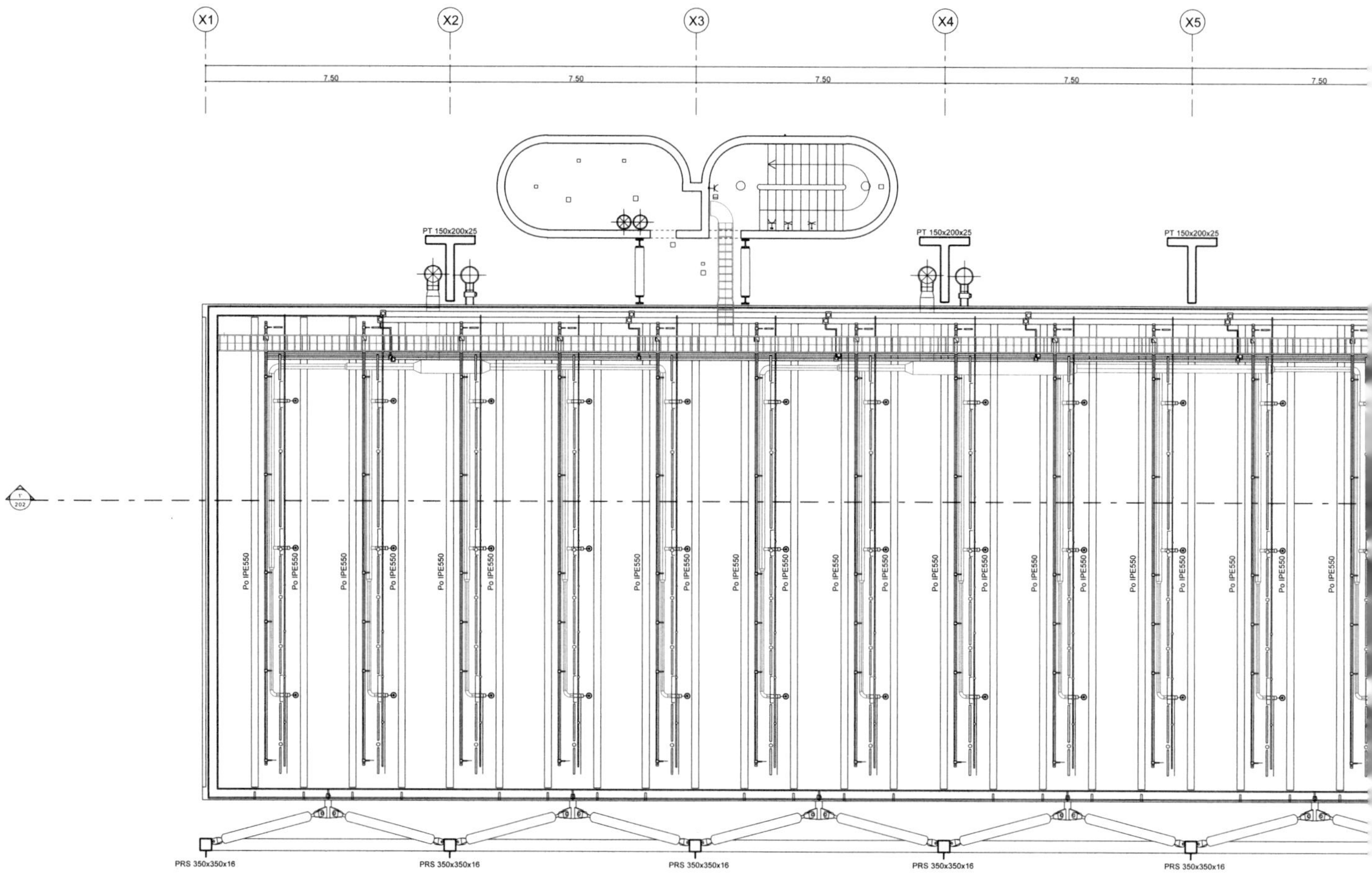
X1
X2
X3
X4
X5
7.50
7.50
7.50
7.50
7.50
PT 150x200x25
PT 150x200x25
PT 150x200x25
Po IPE550
PRS 350x350x16
PRS 350x350x16
PRS 350x350x16
PRS 350x350x16
PRS 350x350x16

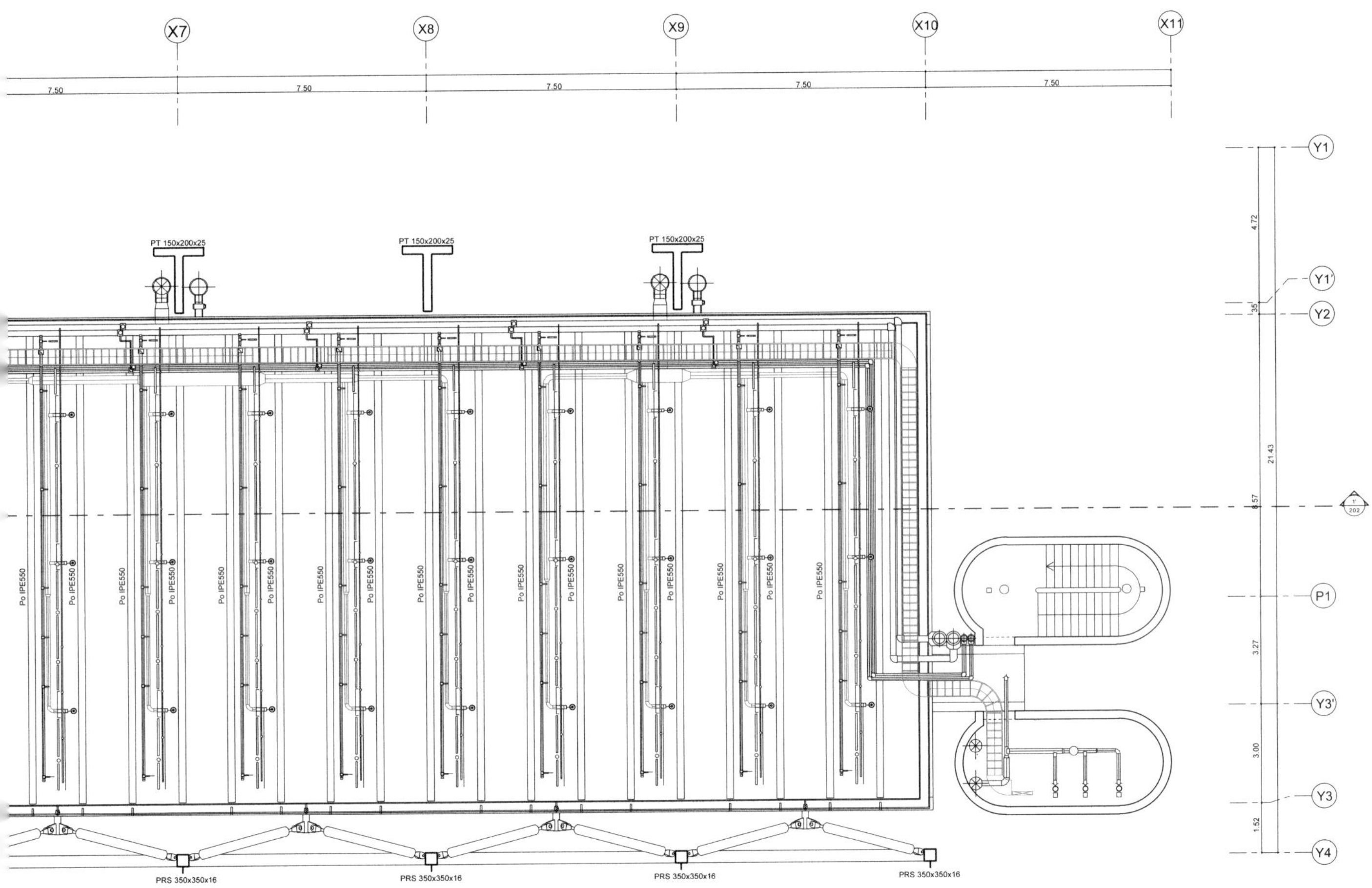
X7
X8
X9
X10
X11
7.50
7.50
7.50
7.50
7.50
PT 150x200x25
PT 150x200x25
PT 150x200x25
Y1
Y1'
Y2
P1
Y3'
Y3
Y4
4.72
35
21.43
3.27
3.00
1.52
Po IPE550
PRS 350x350x16
PRS 350x350x16
PRS 350x350x16
PRS 350x350x16

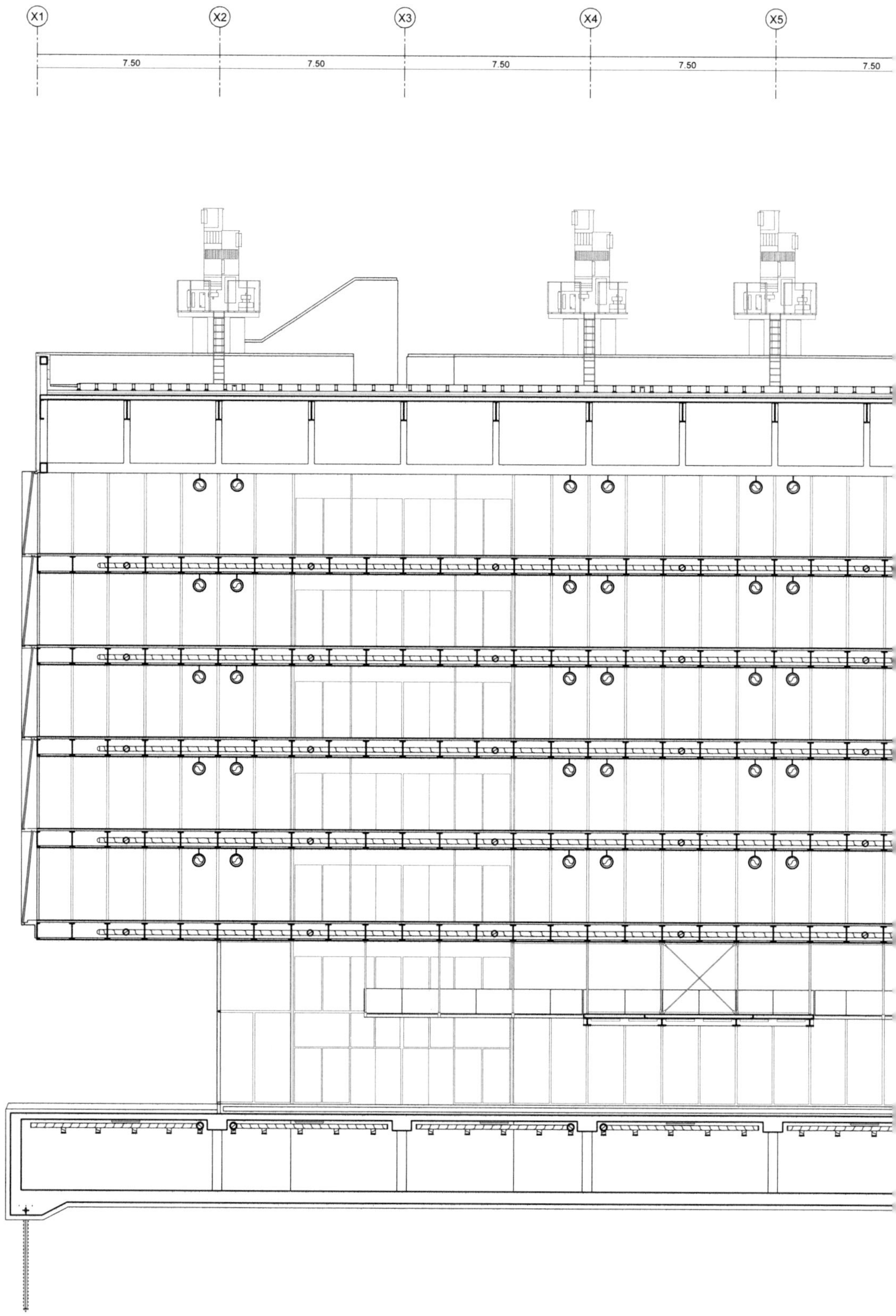
X1
X2
X3
X4
X5
7.50
7.50
7.50
7.50
7.50

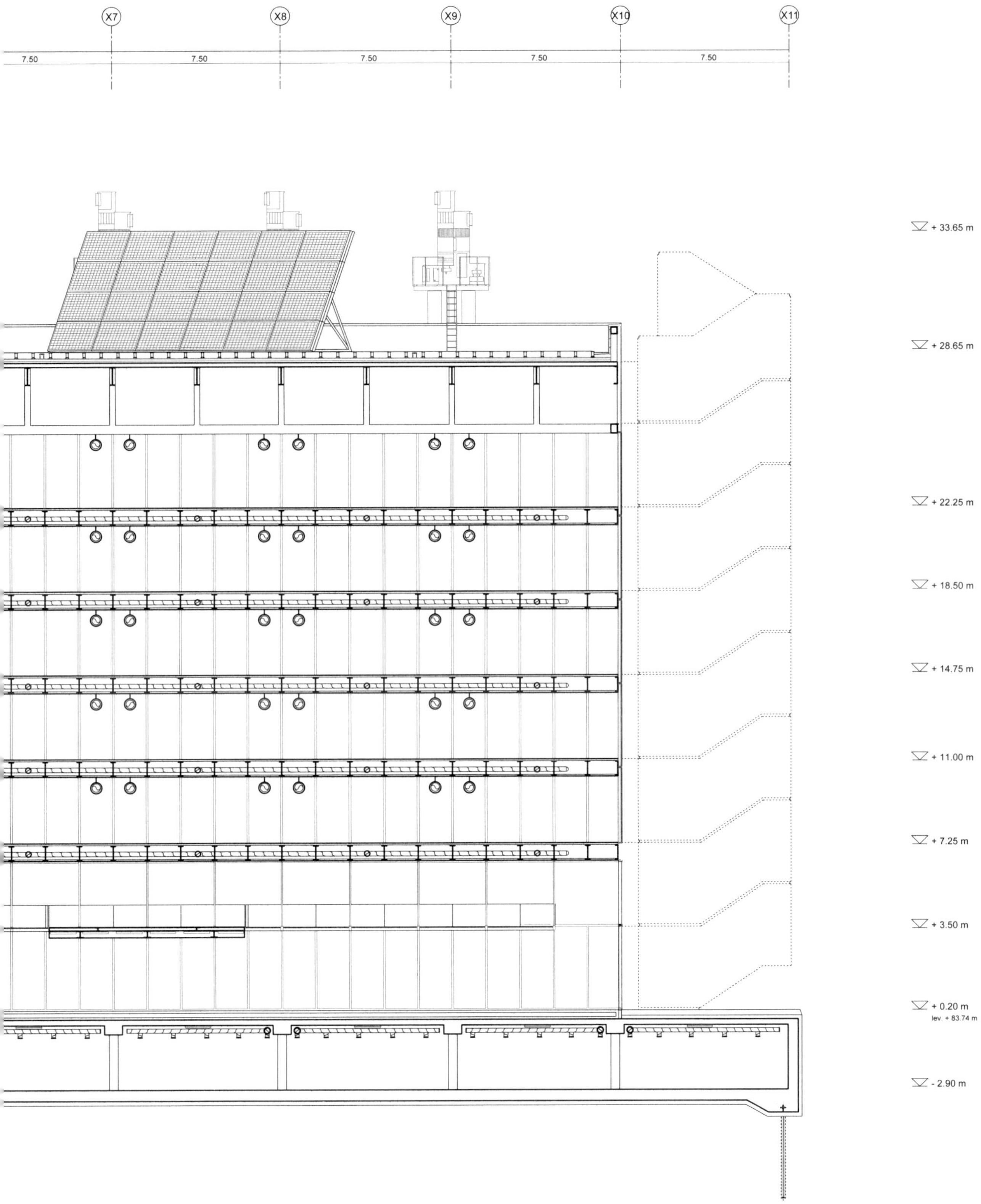
X7
X8
X9
X10
X11
7.50
7.50
7.50
7.50
7.50
+ 33.65 m
+ 28.65 m
+ 22.25 m
+ 18.50 m
+ 14.75 m
+ 11.00 m
+ 7.25 m
+ 3.50 m
+ 0.20 m
lev. + 83.74 m
- 2.90 m

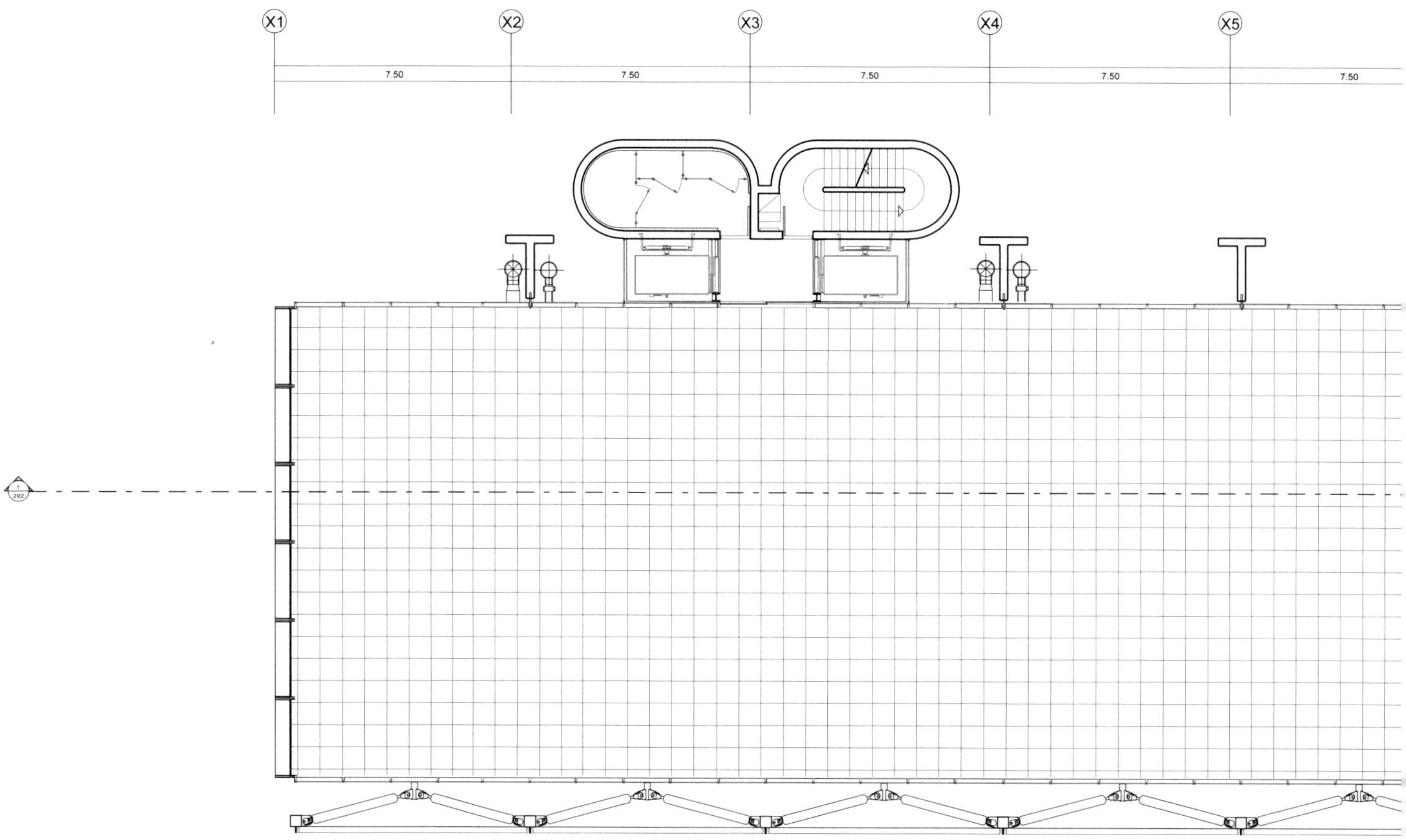
X1
X2
X3
X4
X5
7.50
7.50
7.50
7.50
7.50

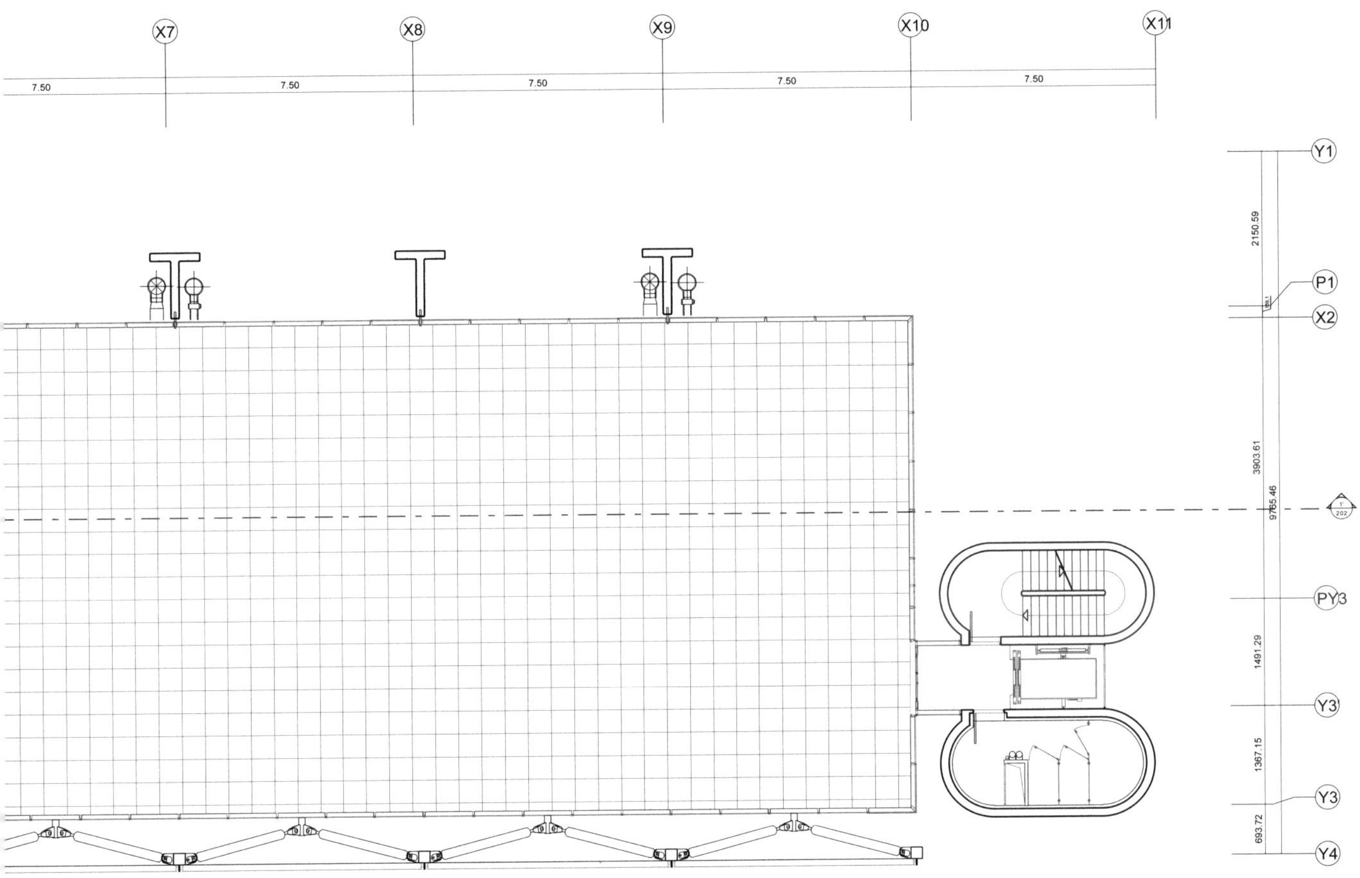
X7
X8
X9
X10
X11
7.50
7.50
7.50
7.50
7.50
Y1
P1
X2
PY3
Y3'
Y3
Y4
2150.59
3903.61
9765.46
1491.29
1367.15
693.72
202

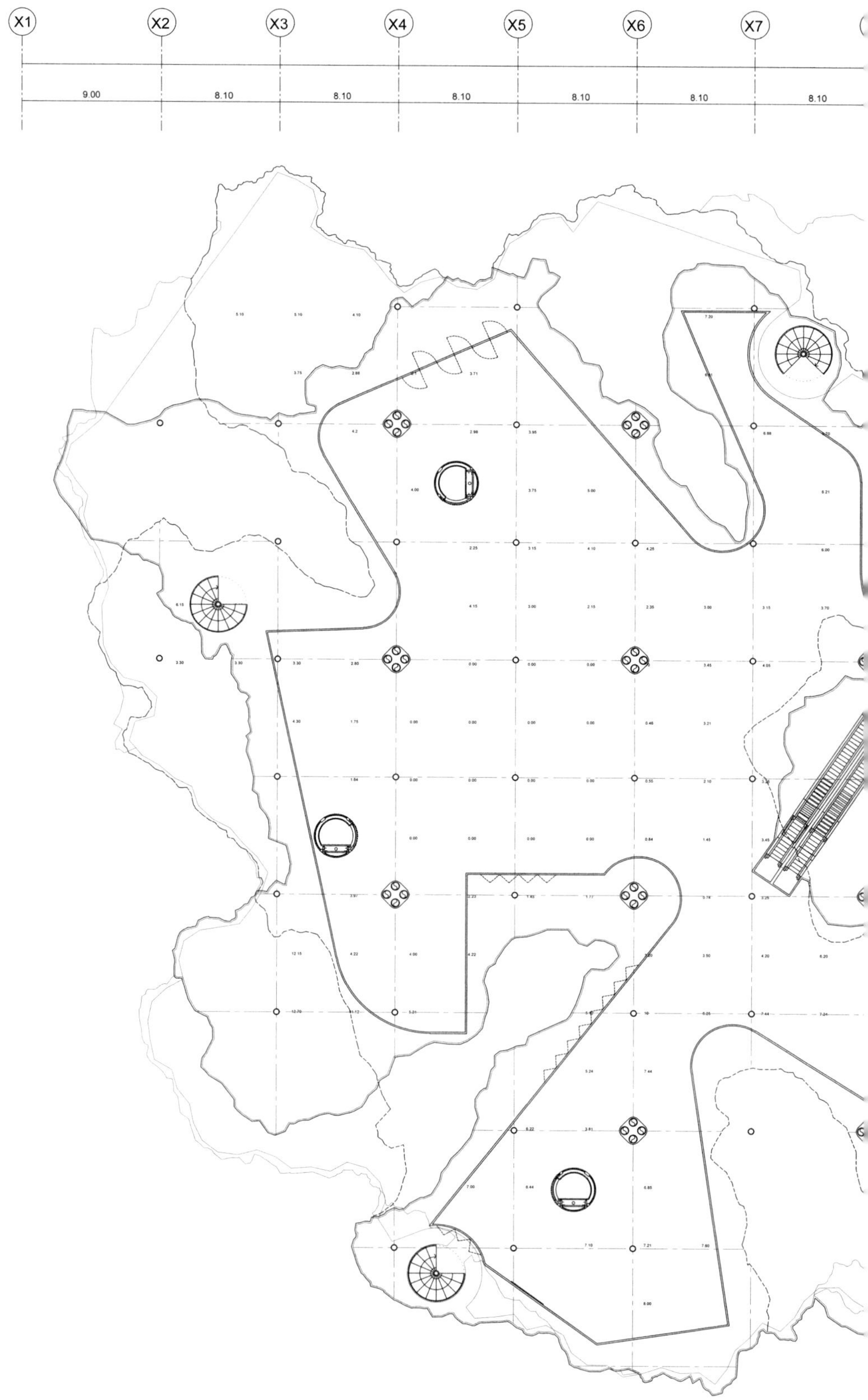

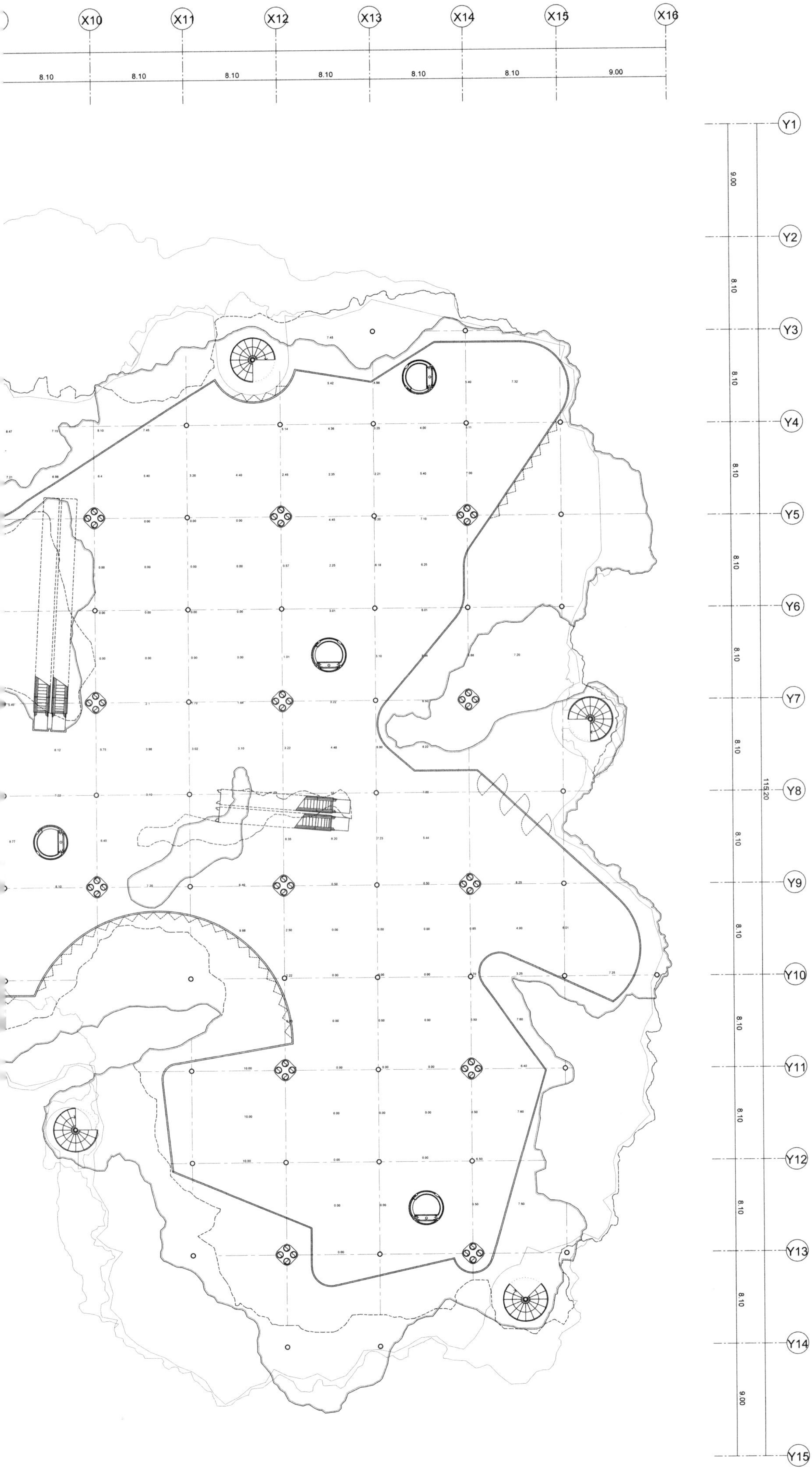

FORUM UZH, Teaching and learning centre

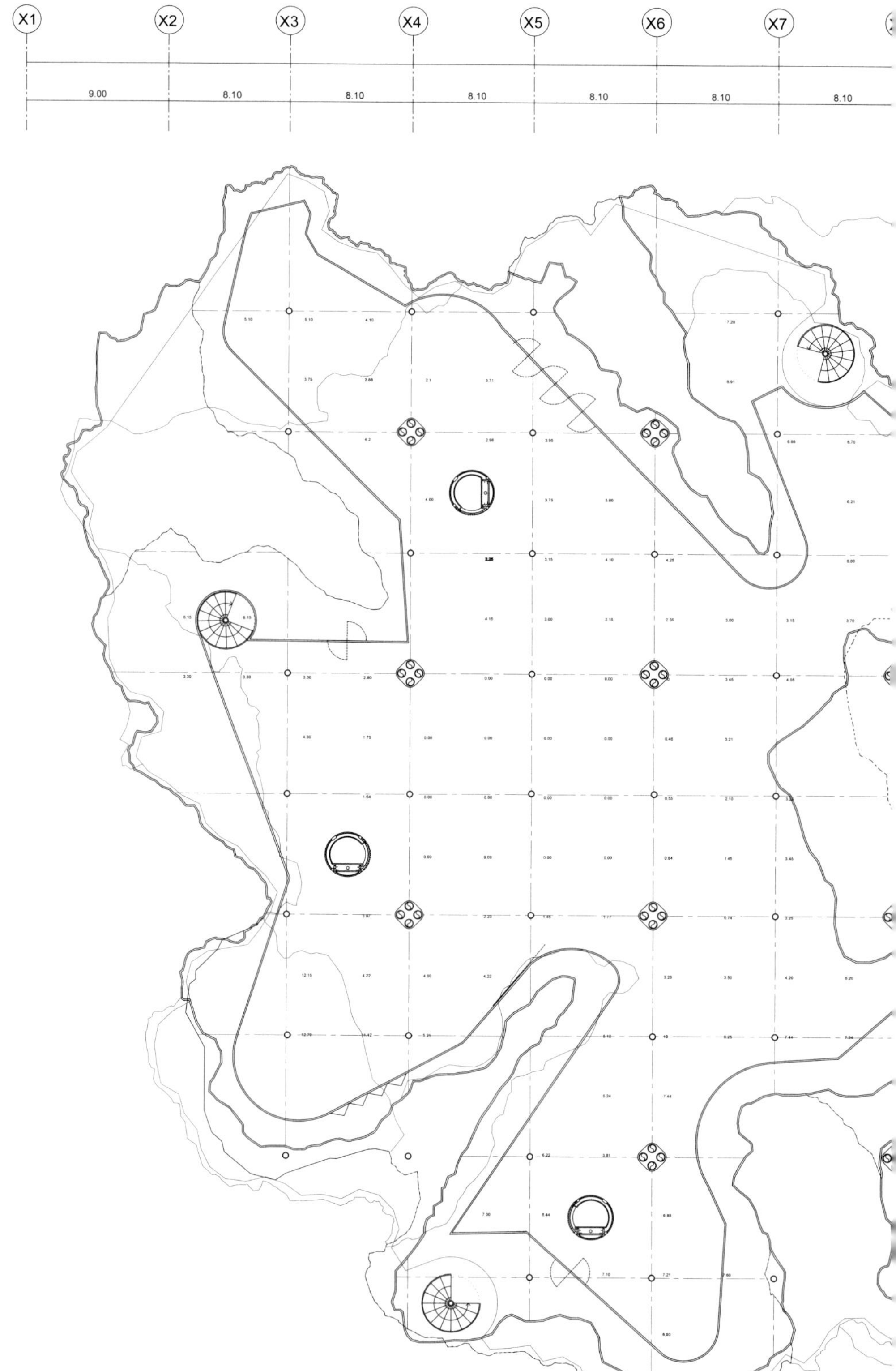

X1
X2
X3
X4
X5
X6
X7
9.00
8.10
8.10
8.10
8.10
8.10
8.10

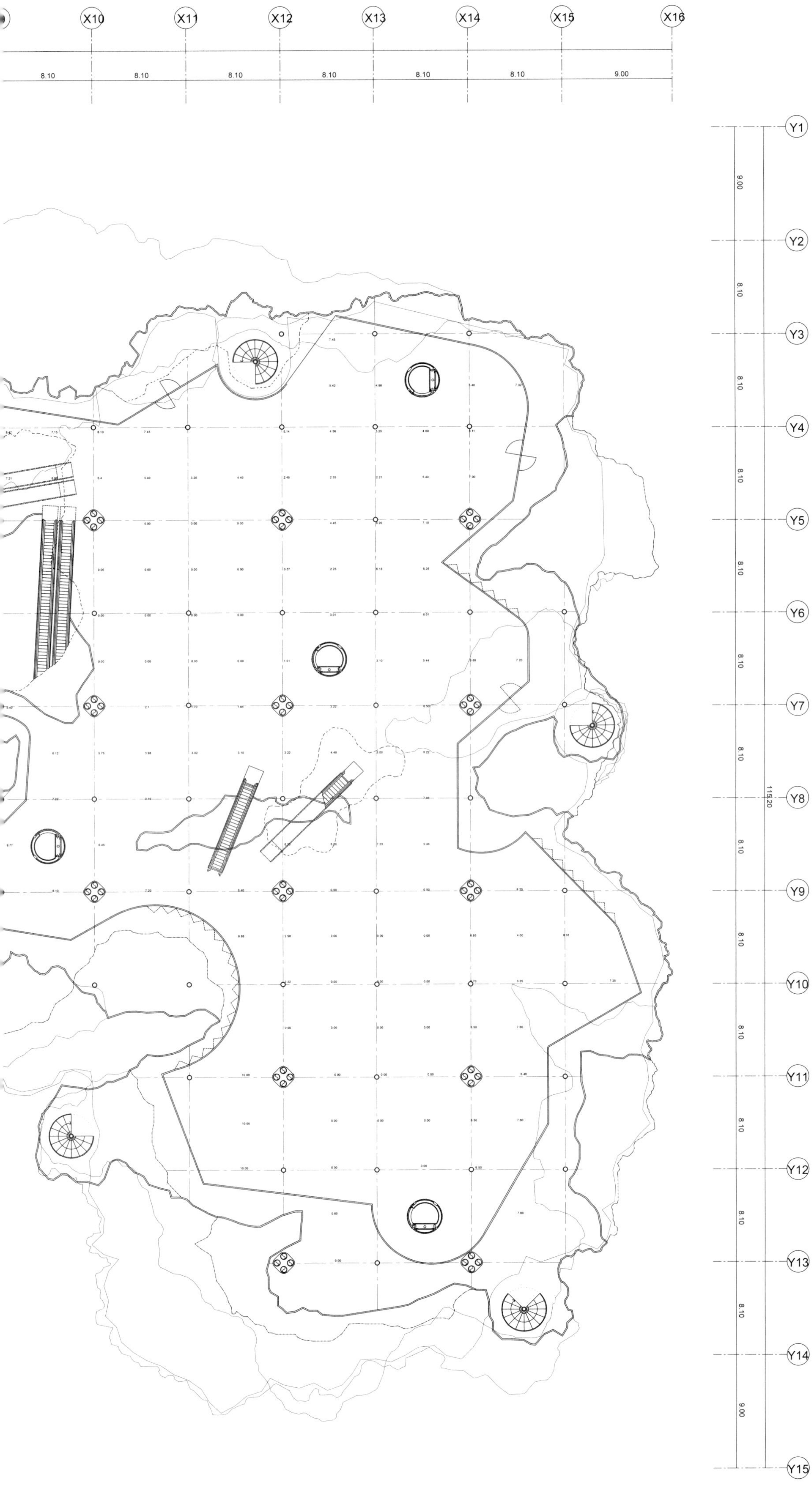
X10
X11
X12
X13
X14
X15
X16
8.10
8.10
8.10
8.10
8.10
8.10
9.00
Y1
Y2
Y3
Y4
Y5
Y6
Y7
Y8
Y9
Y10
Y11
Y12
Y13
Y14
Y15
9.00
8.10
8.10
8.10
8.10
8.10
8.10
8.10
8.10
8.10
8.10
8.10
8.10
9.00
115.20

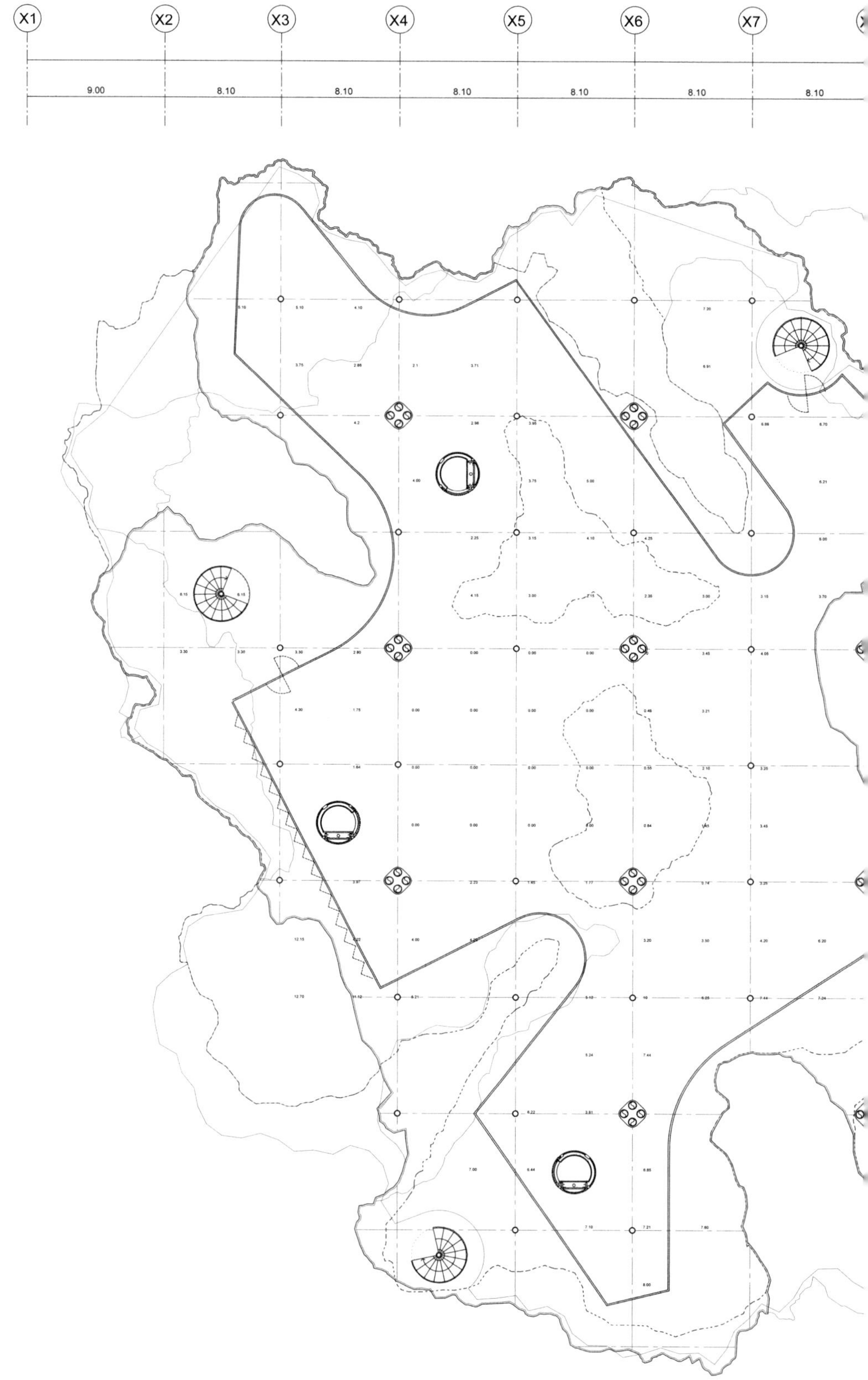
X1
X2
X3
X4
X5
X6
X7
9.00
8.10
8.10
8.10
8.10
8.10
8.10

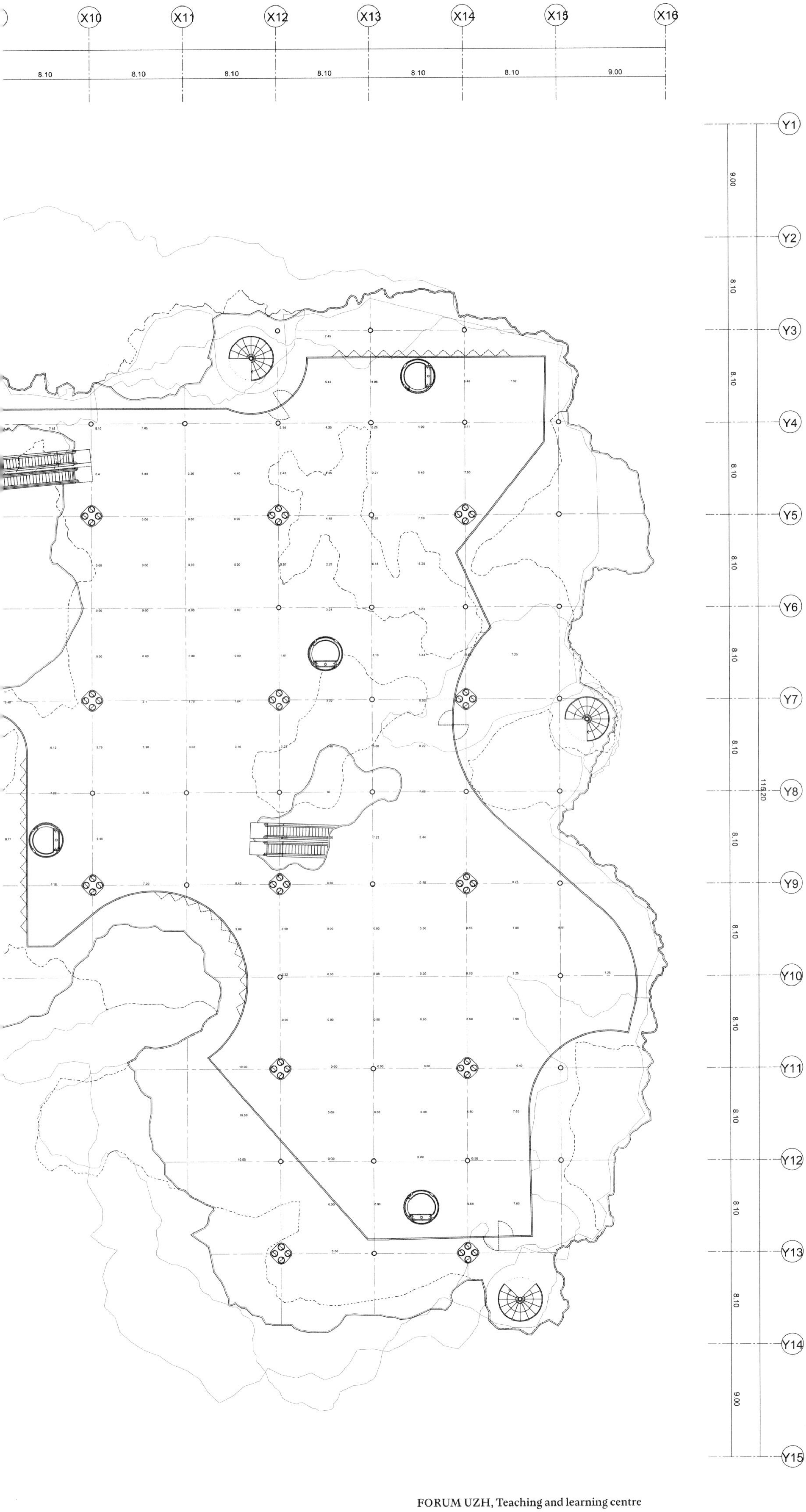
X10
X11
X12
X13
X14
X15
X16
8.10
8.10
8.10
8.10
8.10
8.10
9.00
Y1
Y2
Y3
Y4
Y5
Y6
Y7
Y8
Y9
Y10
Y11
Y12
Y13
Y14
Y15
115.20

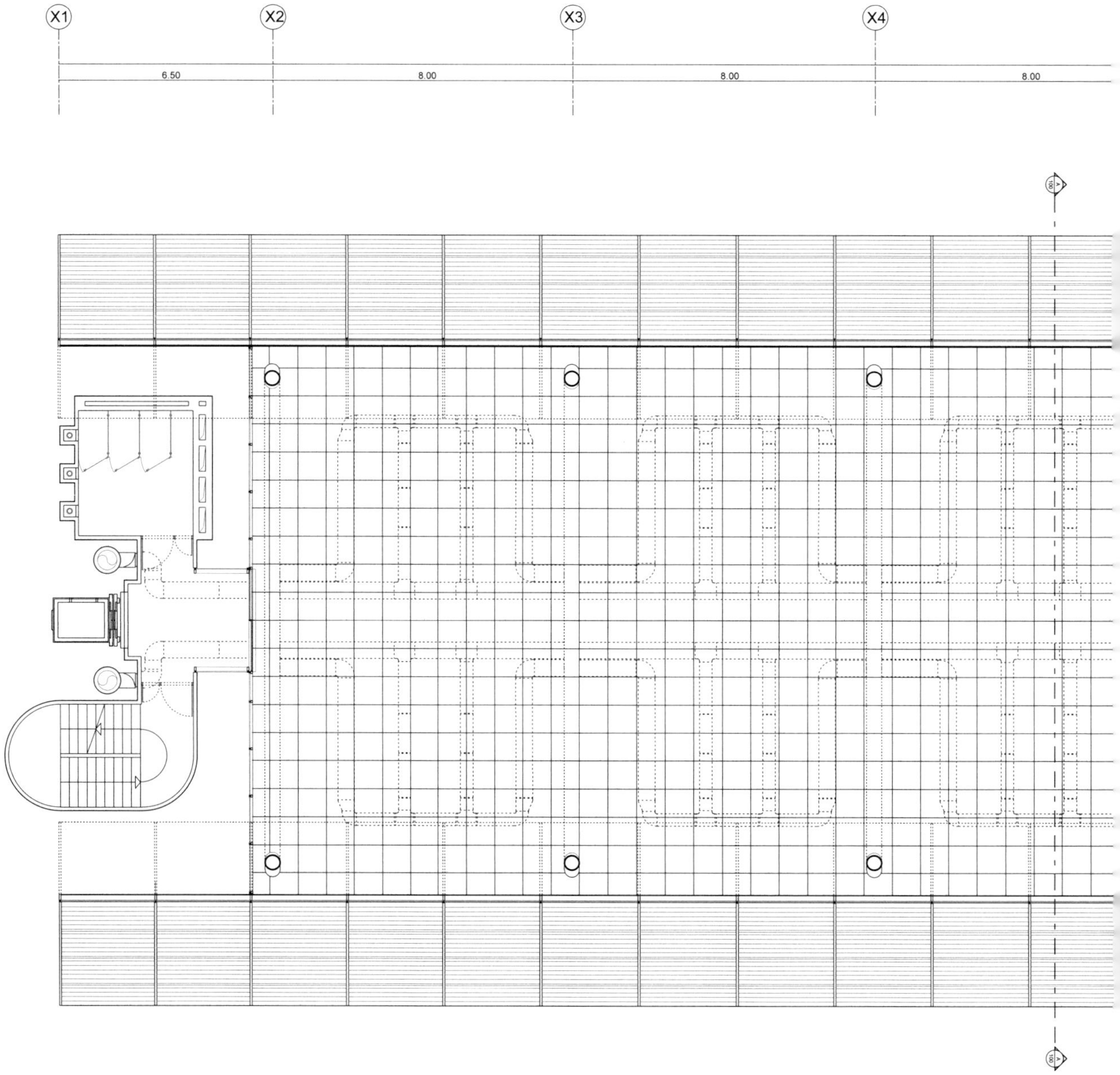
X1
X2
X3
X4
6.50
8.00
8.00
8.00

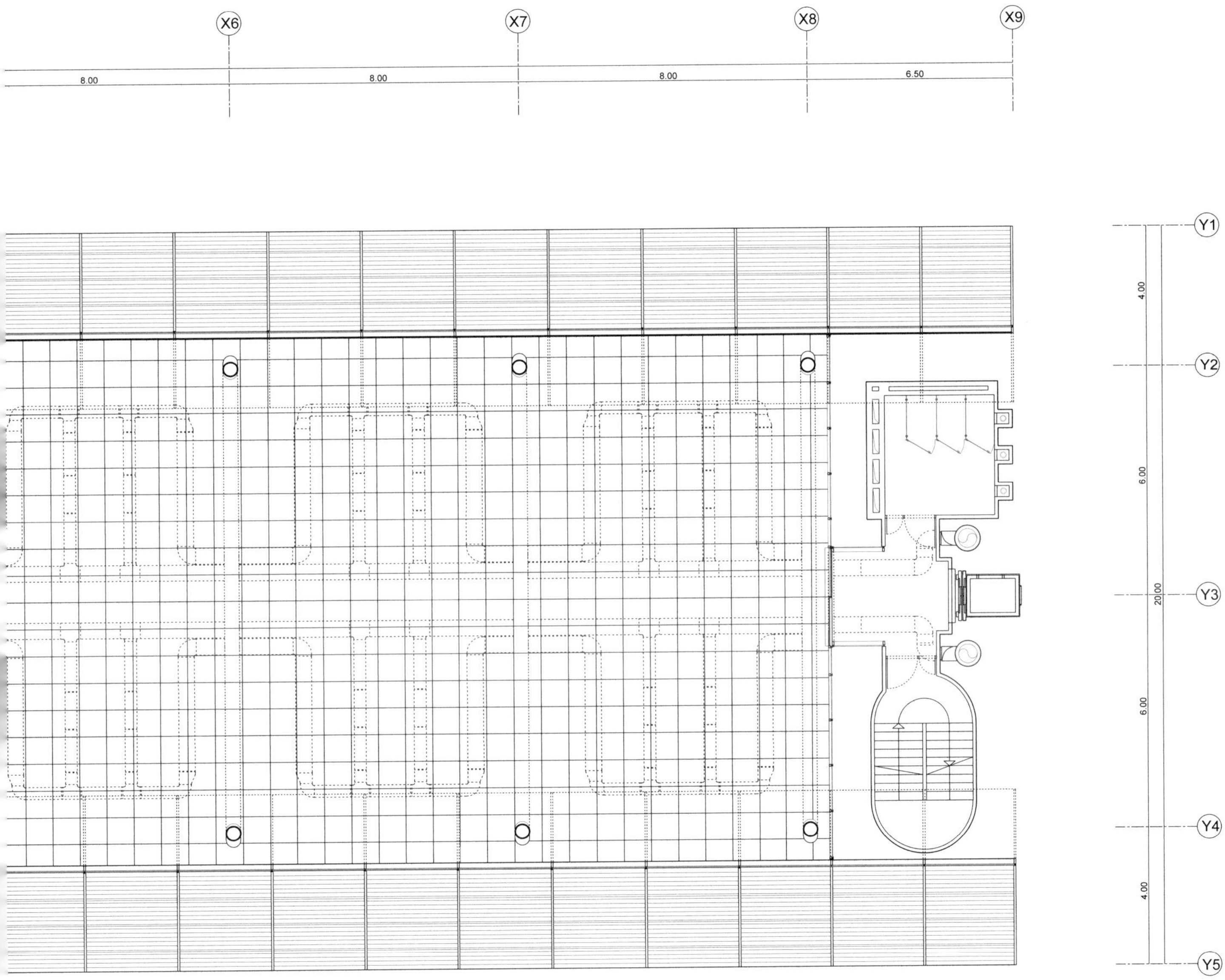
X6
X7
X8
X9
8.00
8.00
8.00
6.50
Y1
Y2
Y3
Y4
Y5
4.00
6.00
20.00
6.00
4.00

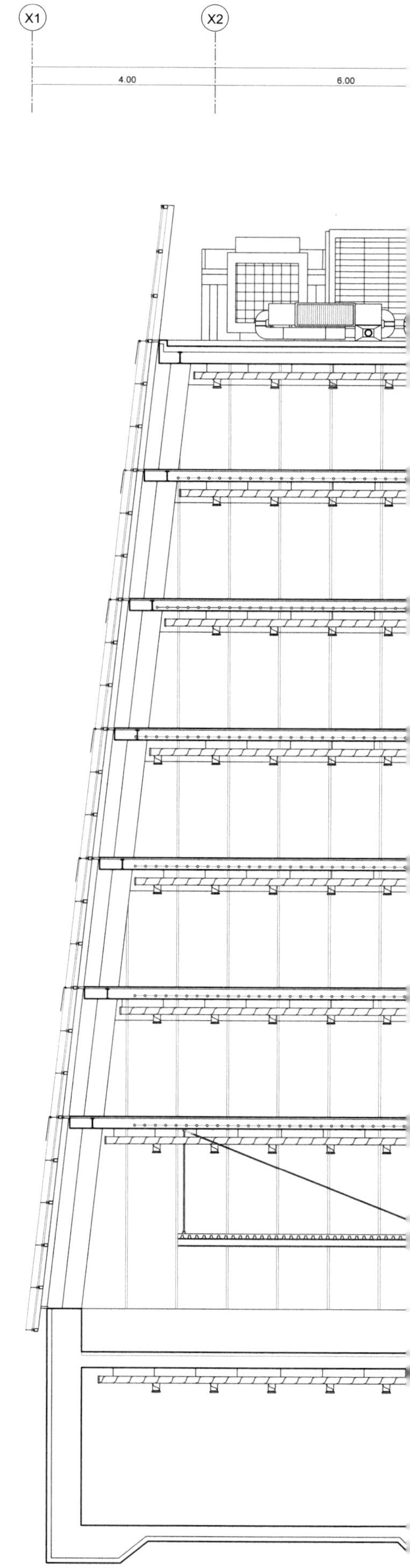
X1
X2
4.00
6.00

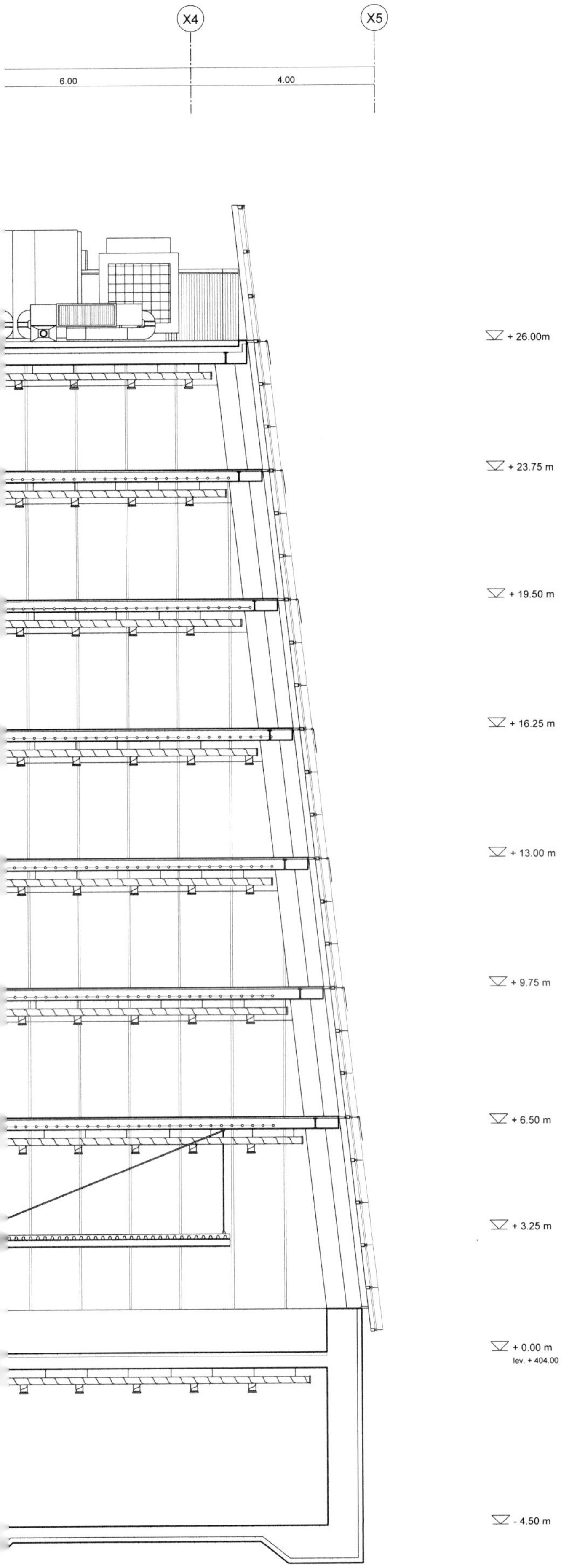
X4
X5
6.00
4.00
+ 26.00m
+ 23.75 m
+ 19.50 m
+ 16.25 m
+ 13.00 m
+ 9.75 m
+ 6.50 m
+ 3.25 m
+ 0.00 m
lev. + 404.00
- 4.50 m

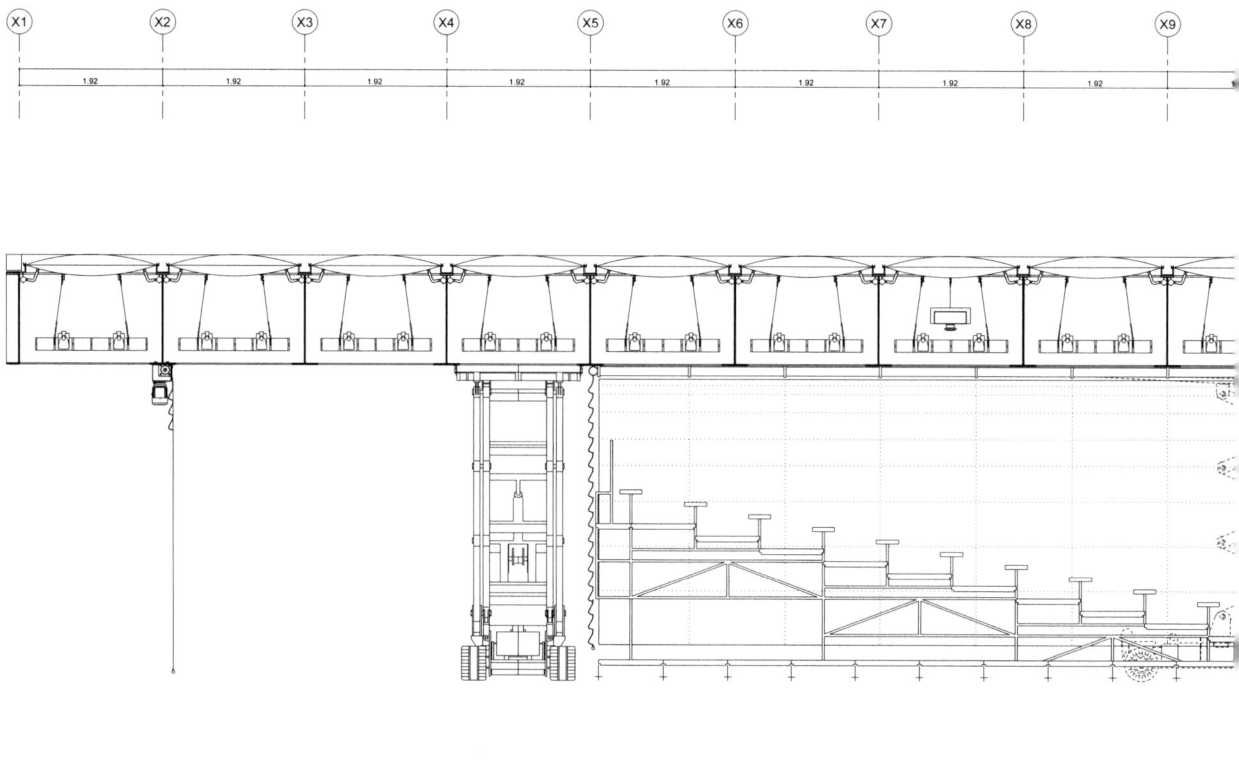
X1
X2
X3
X4
X5
X6
X7
X8
X9
1.92
1.92
1.92
1.92
1.92
1.92
1.92
1.92

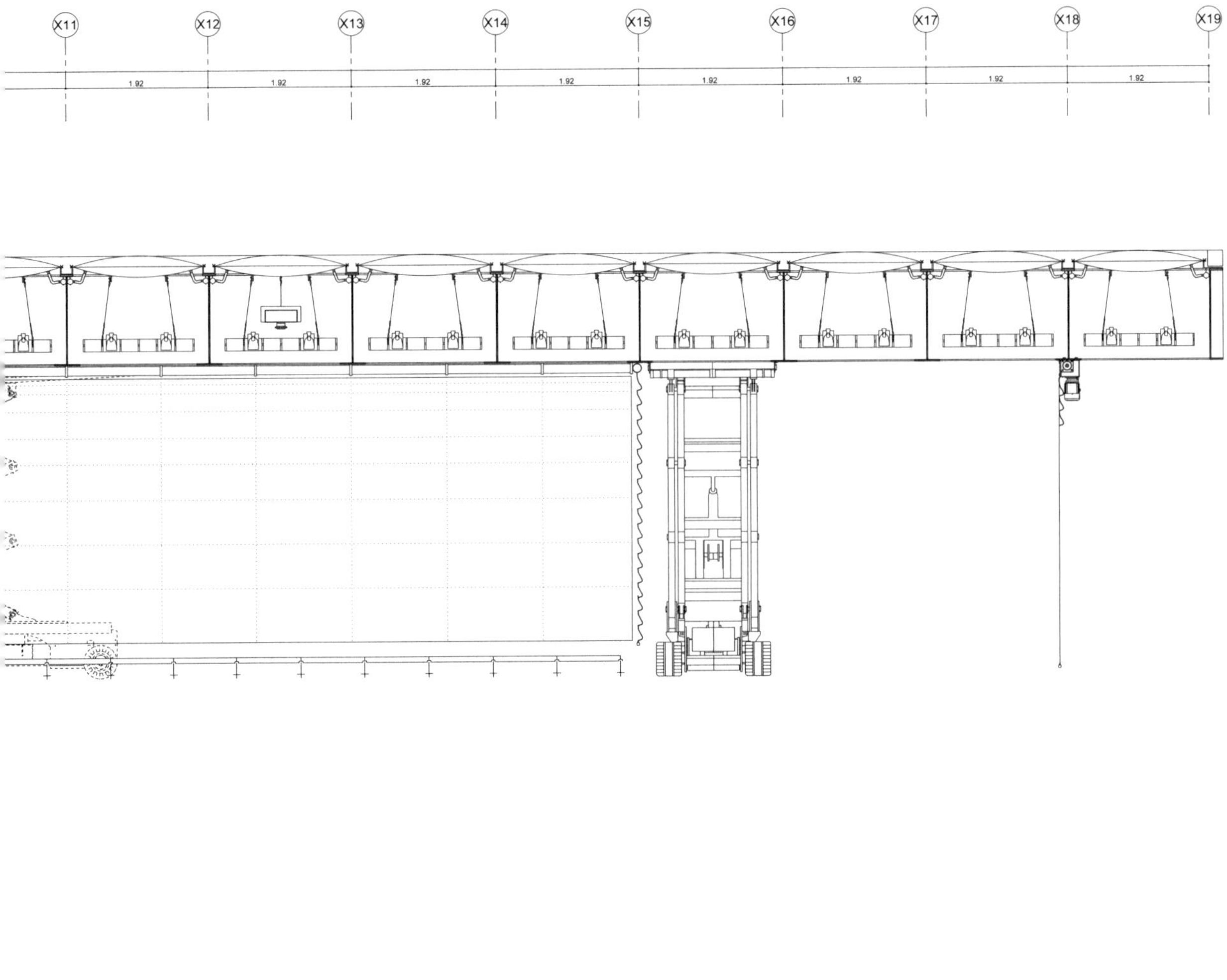
X11
X12
X13
X14
X15
X16
X17
X18
X19
1.92
1.92
1.92
1.92
1.92
1.92
1.92
1.92

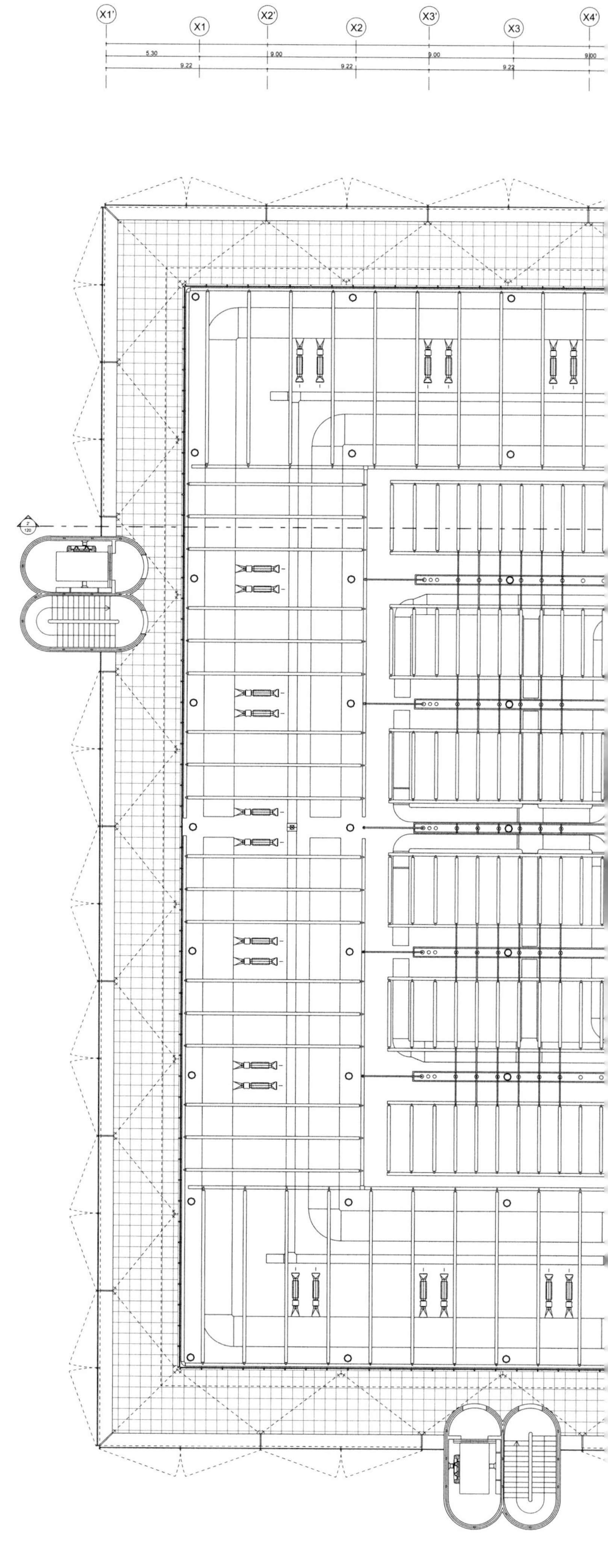
X1'
X1
X2'
X2
X3'
X3
X4'
5.30
9.00
9.00
9.00
9.22
9.22
9.22

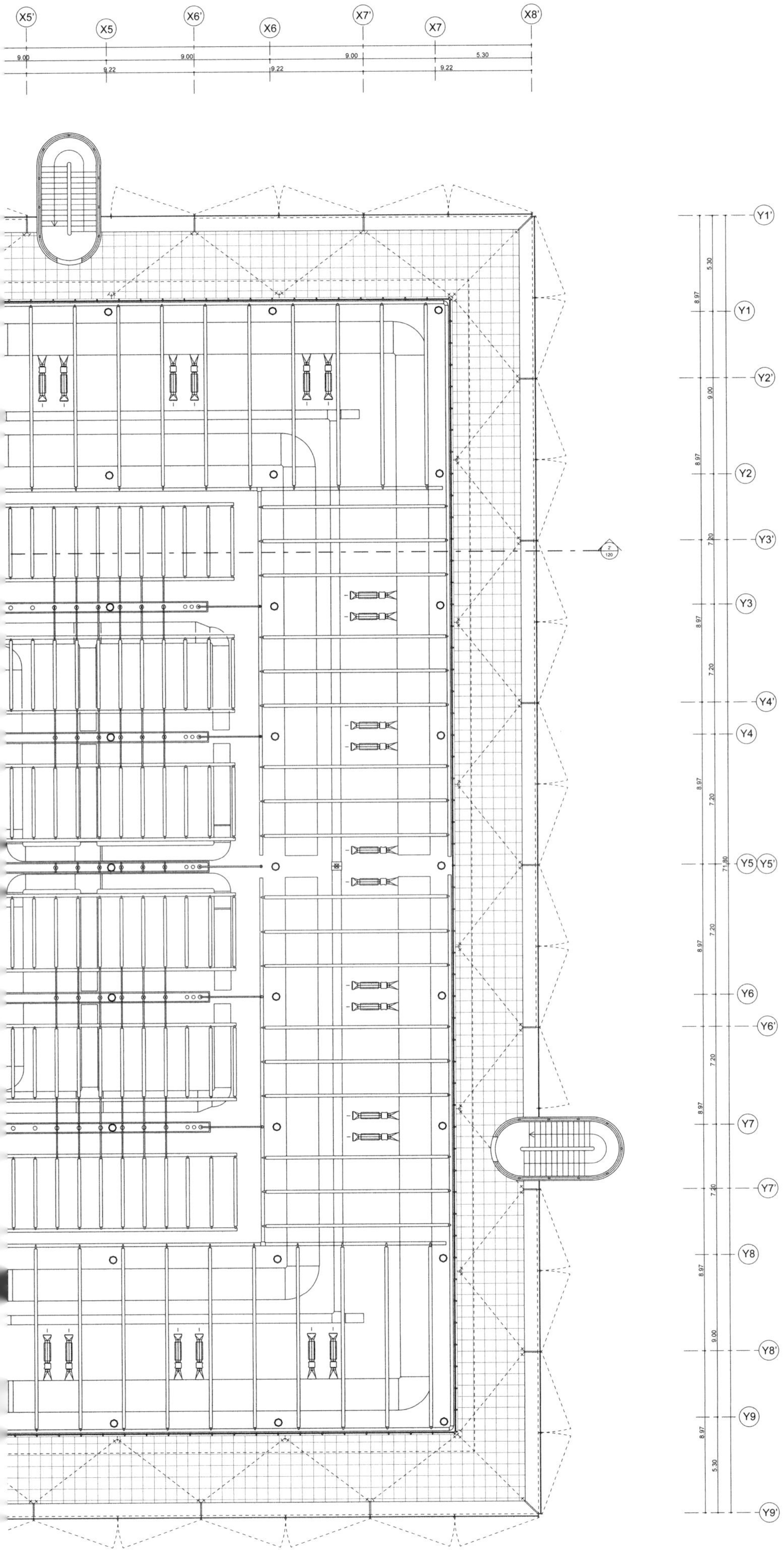
X5'
X5
X6'
X6
X7'
X7
X8'
Y1'
Y1
Y2'
Y2
Y3'
Y3
Y4'
Y4
Y5
Y5'
Y6
Y6'
Y7
Y7'
Y8
Y8'
Y9
Y9'

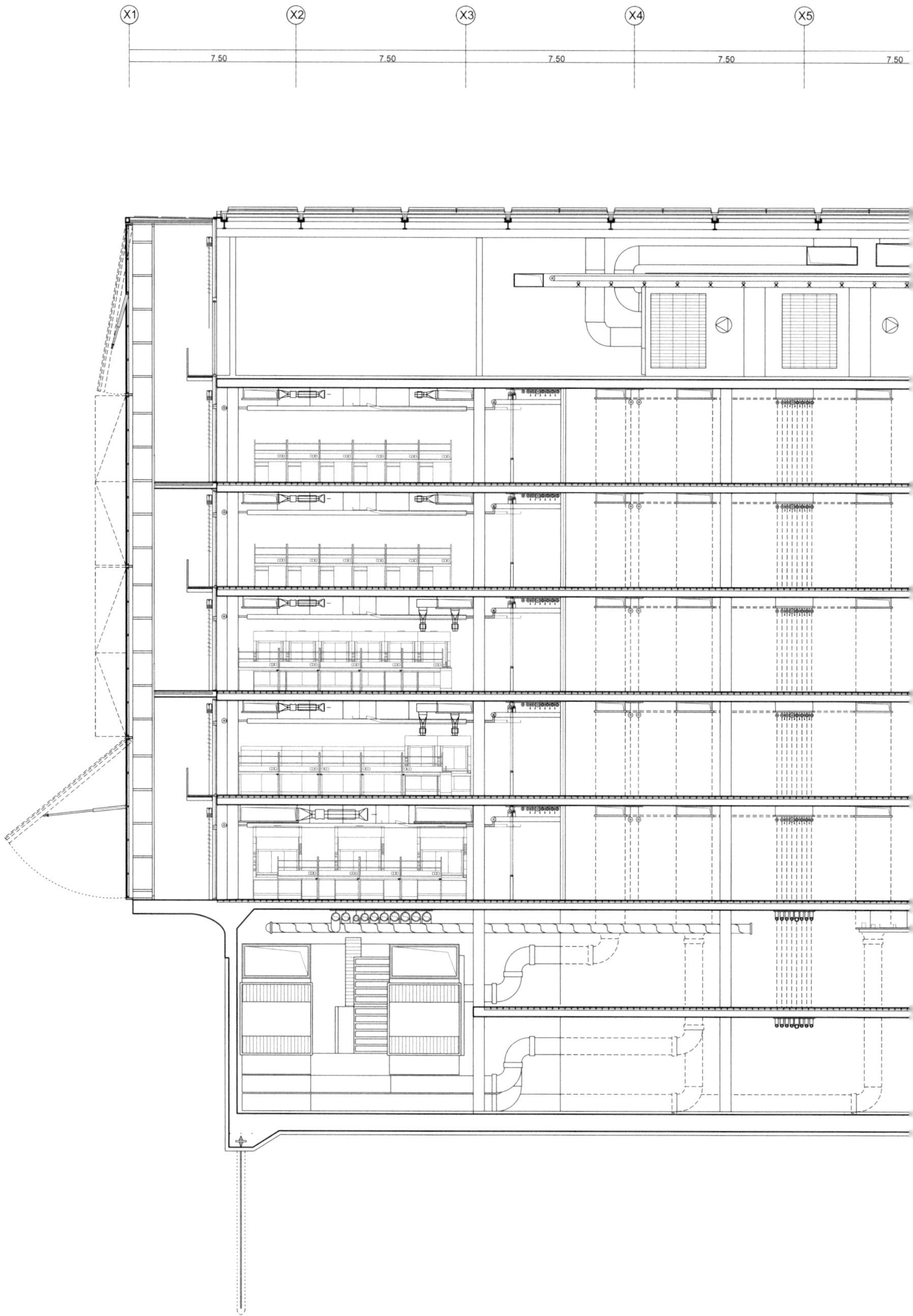

X1
X2
X3
X4
X5
7.50
7.50
7.50
7.50
7.50

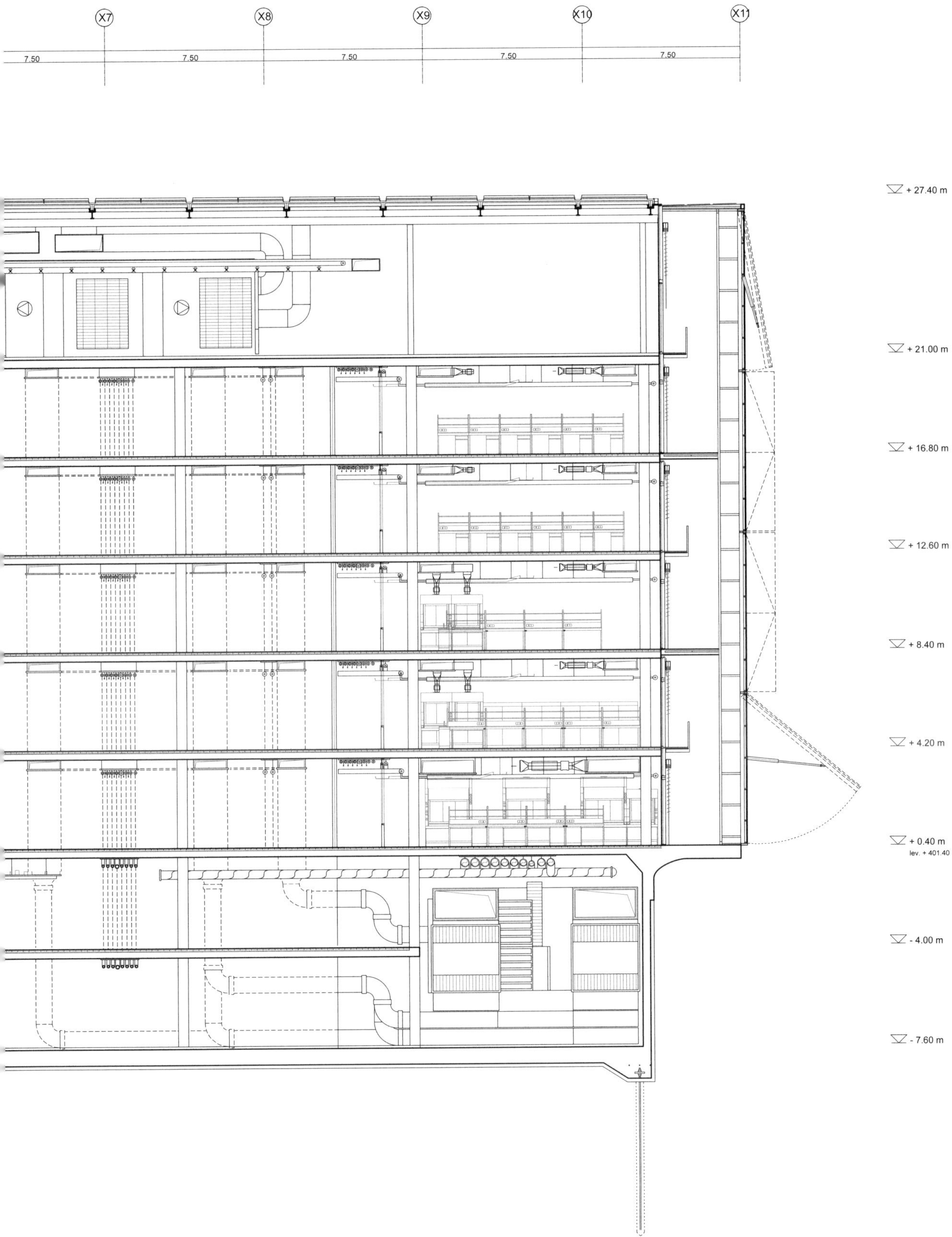
X7
X8
X9
X10
X11
7.50
7.50
7.50
7.50
7.50
+ 27.40 m
+ 21.00 m
+ 16.80 m
+ 12.60 m
+ 8.40 m
+ 4.20 m
+ 0.40 m
lev. + 401.40
- 4.00 m
- 7.60 m

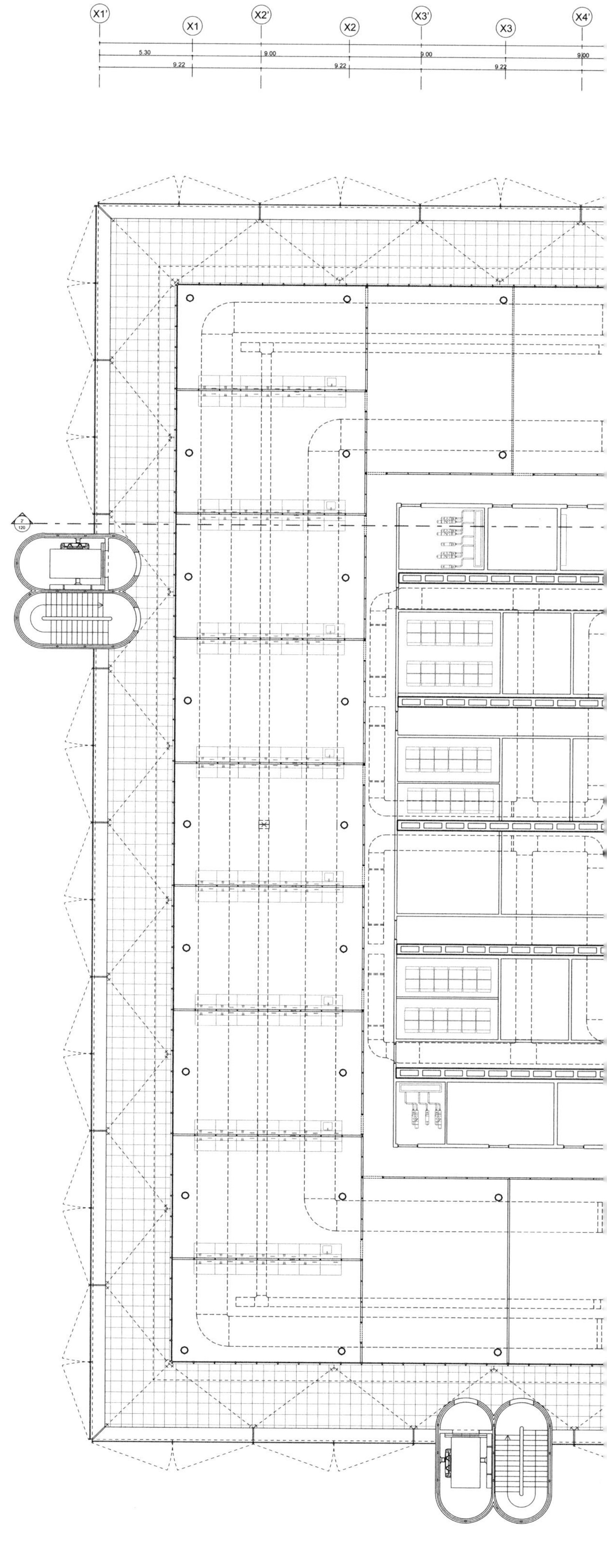
X1'
X1
X2'
X2
X3'
X3
X4'
5.30
9.22
9.00
9.22
9.00
9.22
9.00

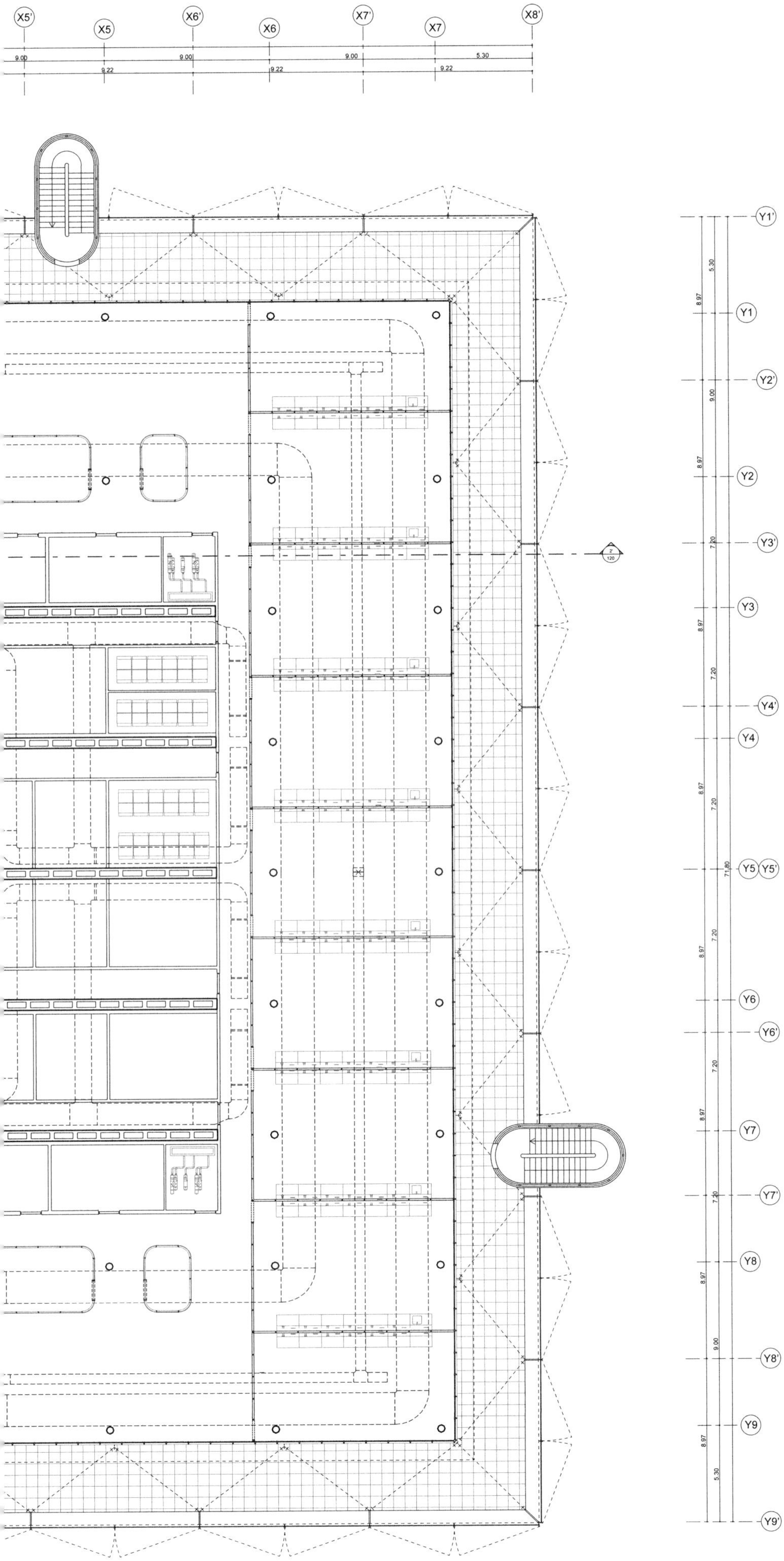

SCIENCES DE LA VIE, Microbiology and neuroscience research and teaching laboratories

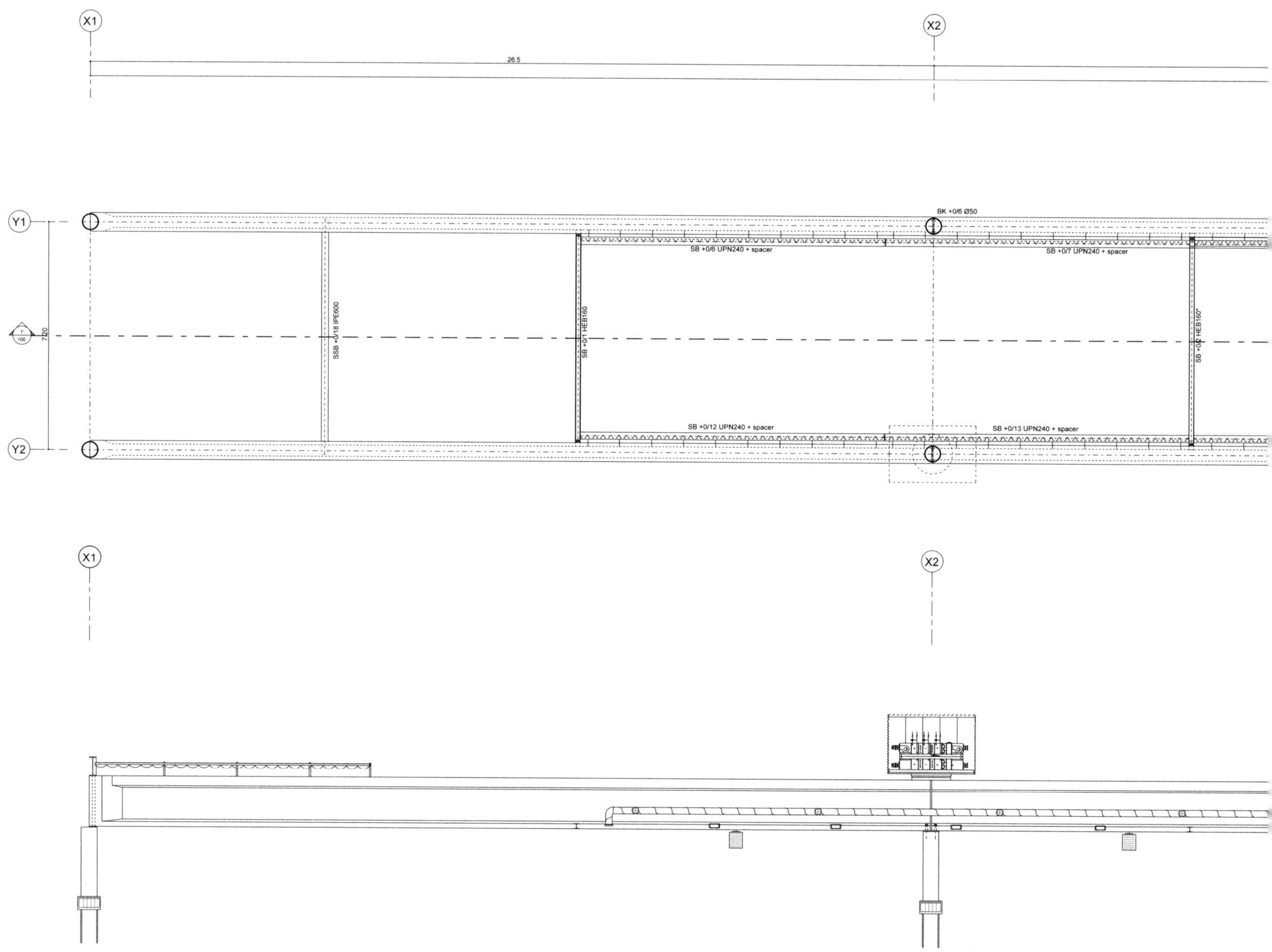

X1
X2
26.5
Y1
Y2
7.20
BK +0/6 Ø50
SB +0/6 UPN240 + spacer
SB +0/7 UPN240 + spacer
SSB +0/18 IPE600
SB +0/12 UPN240 + spacer
SB +0/13 UPN240 + spacer

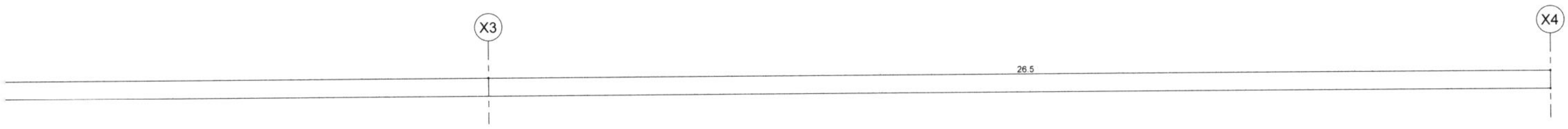
X3
X4
26.5

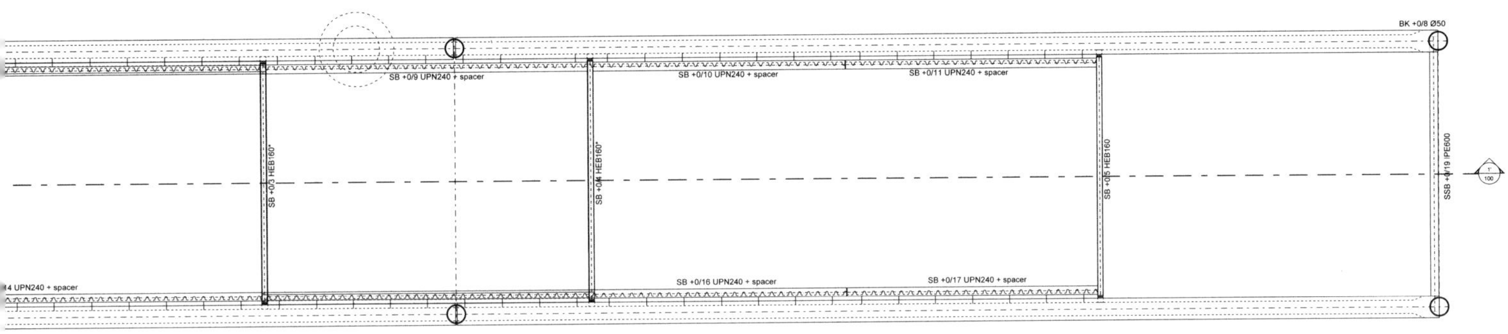
BK +0/8 Ø50
SB +0/9 UPN240 + spacer
SB +0/10 UPN240 + spacer
SB +0/11 UPN240 + spacer
SB +0/16 UPN240 + spacer
SB +0/17 UPN240 + spacer
4 UPN240 + spacer

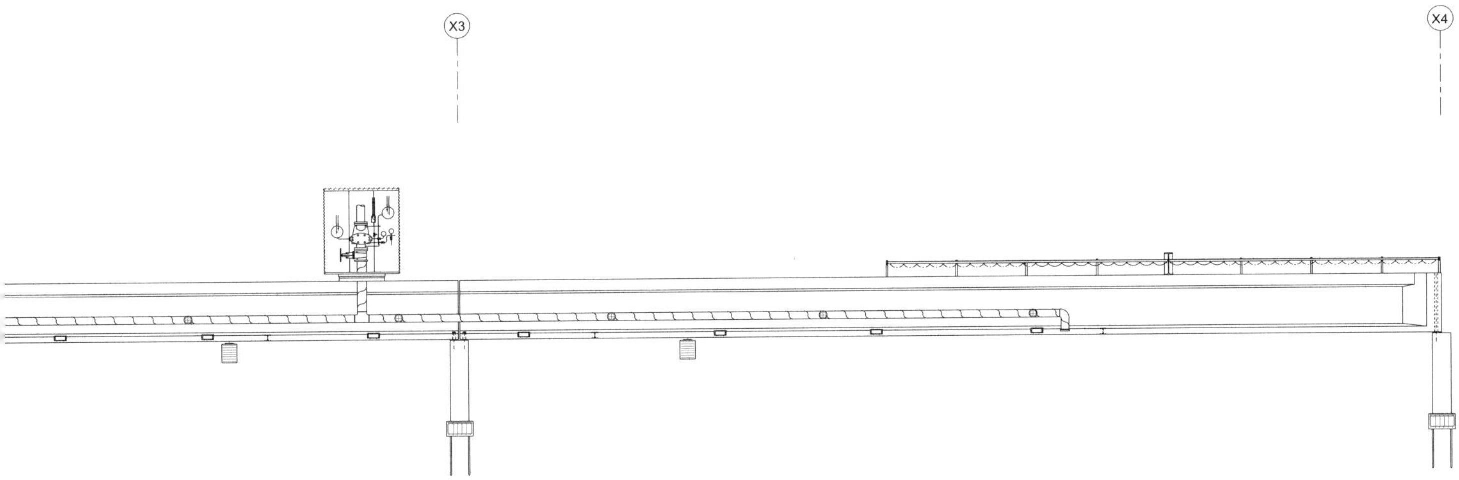
X3
X4

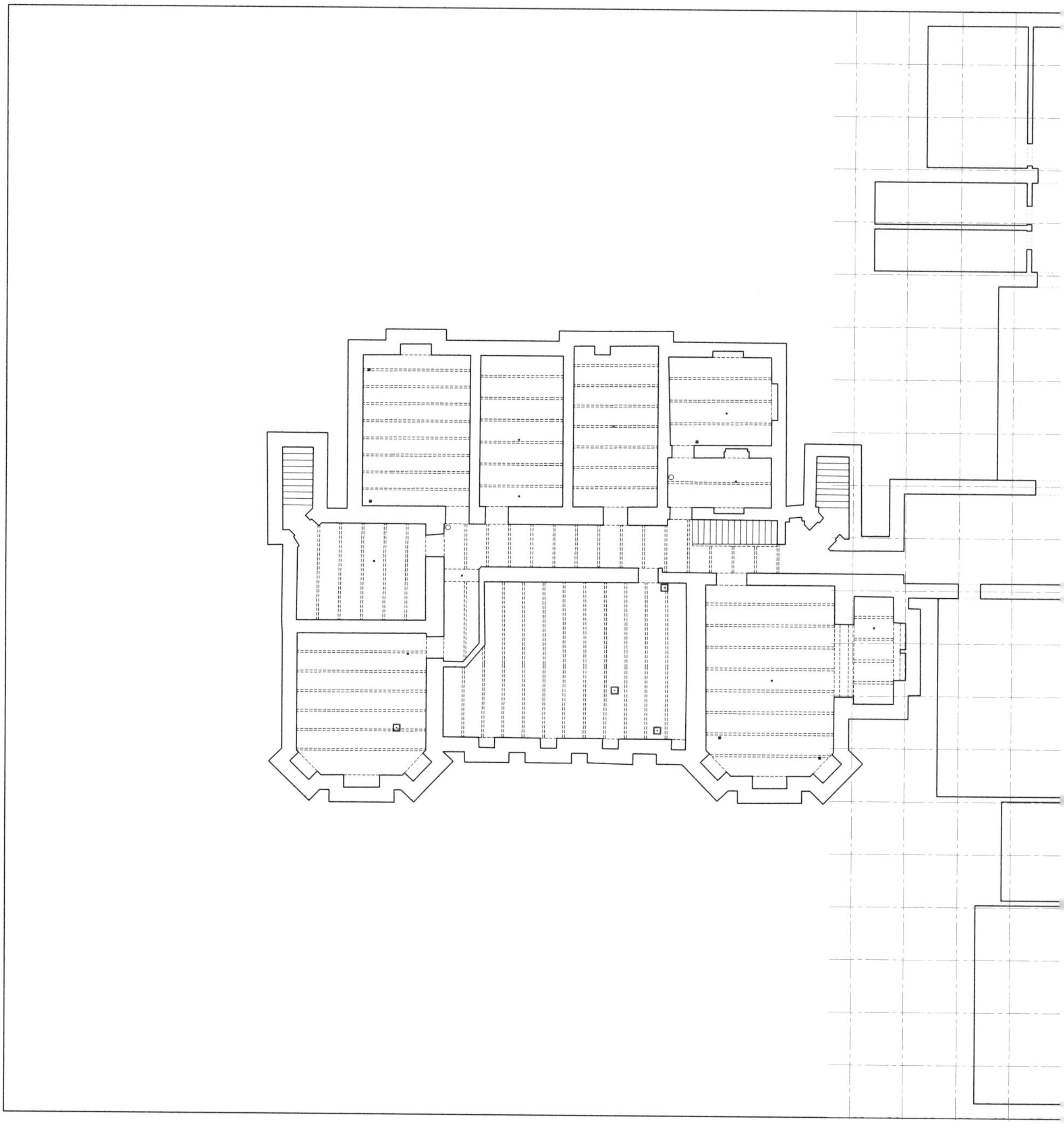

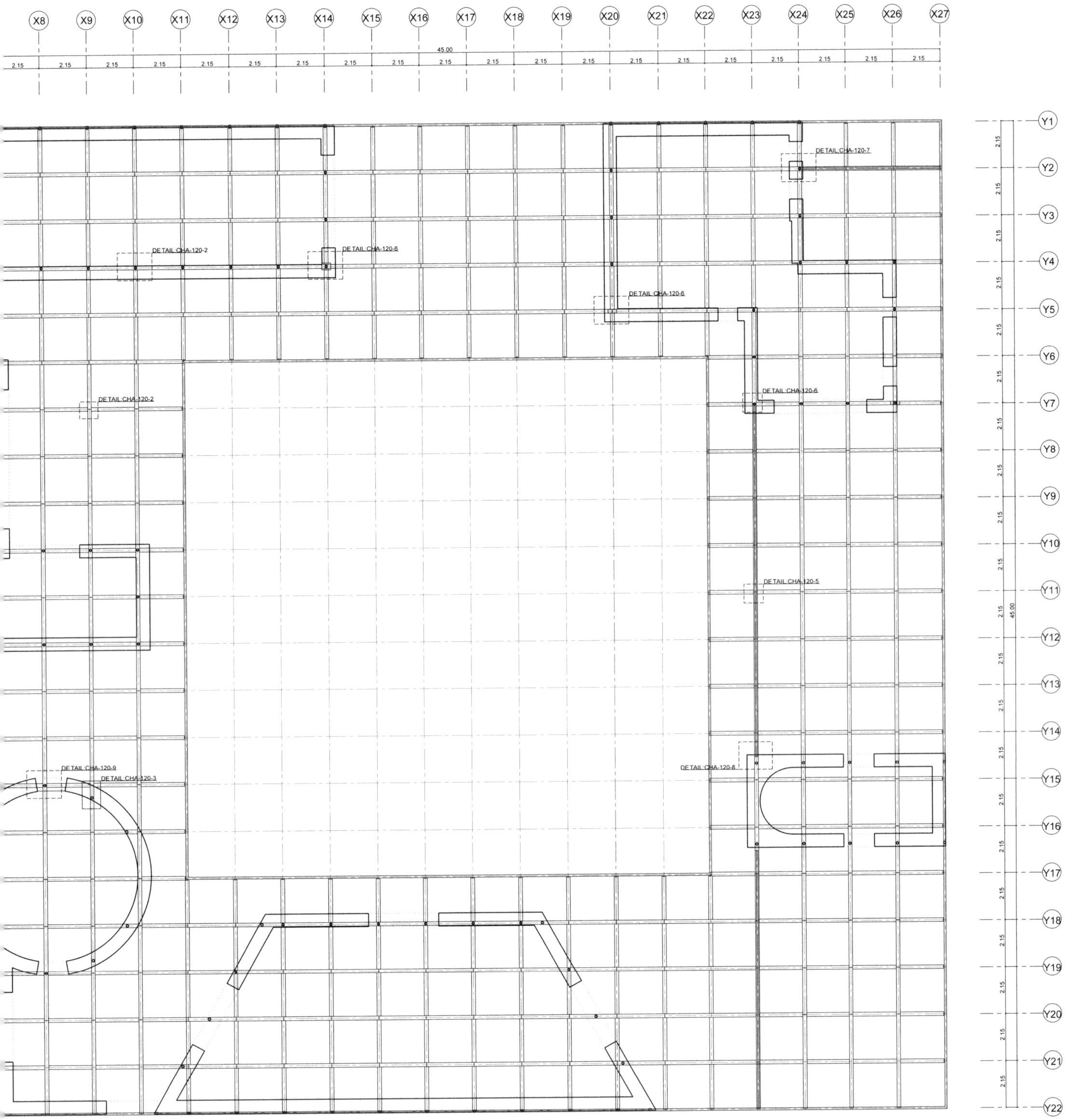
X8
X9
X10
X11
X12
X13
X14
X15
X16
X17
X18
X19
X20
X21
X22
X23
X24
X25
X26
X27
45.00
2.15
Y1
Y2
Y3
Y4
Y5
Y6
Y7
Y8
Y9
Y10
Y11
Y12
Y13
Y14
Y15
Y16
Y17
Y18
Y19
Y20
Y21
Y22
DETAIL CHA-120-7
DETAIL CHA-120-2
DETAIL CHA-120-6
DETAIL CHA-120-5
DETAIL CHA-120-9
DETAIL CHA-120-3
DETAIL CHA-120-8

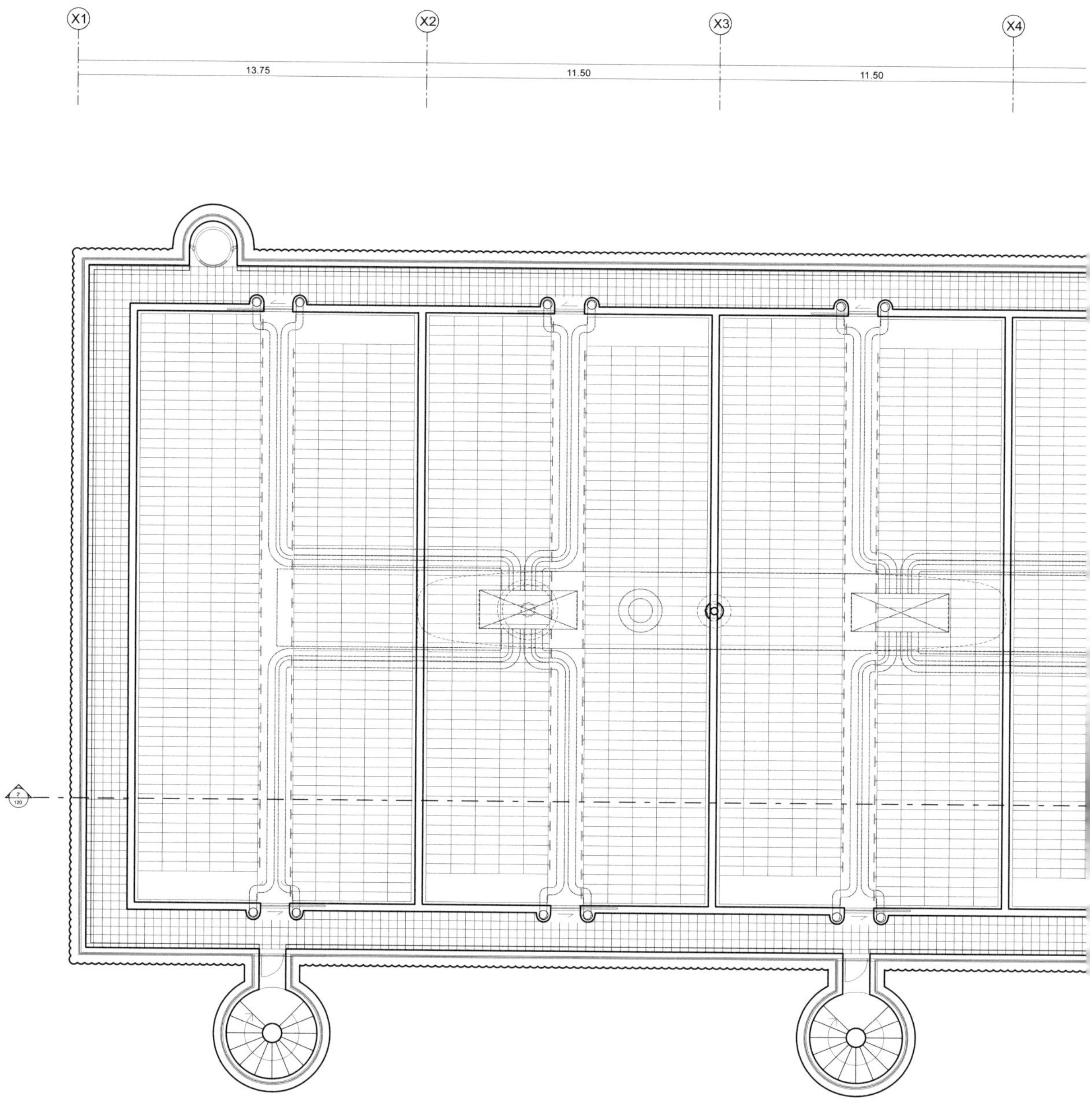

X1
X2
X3
X4
13.75
11.50
11.50

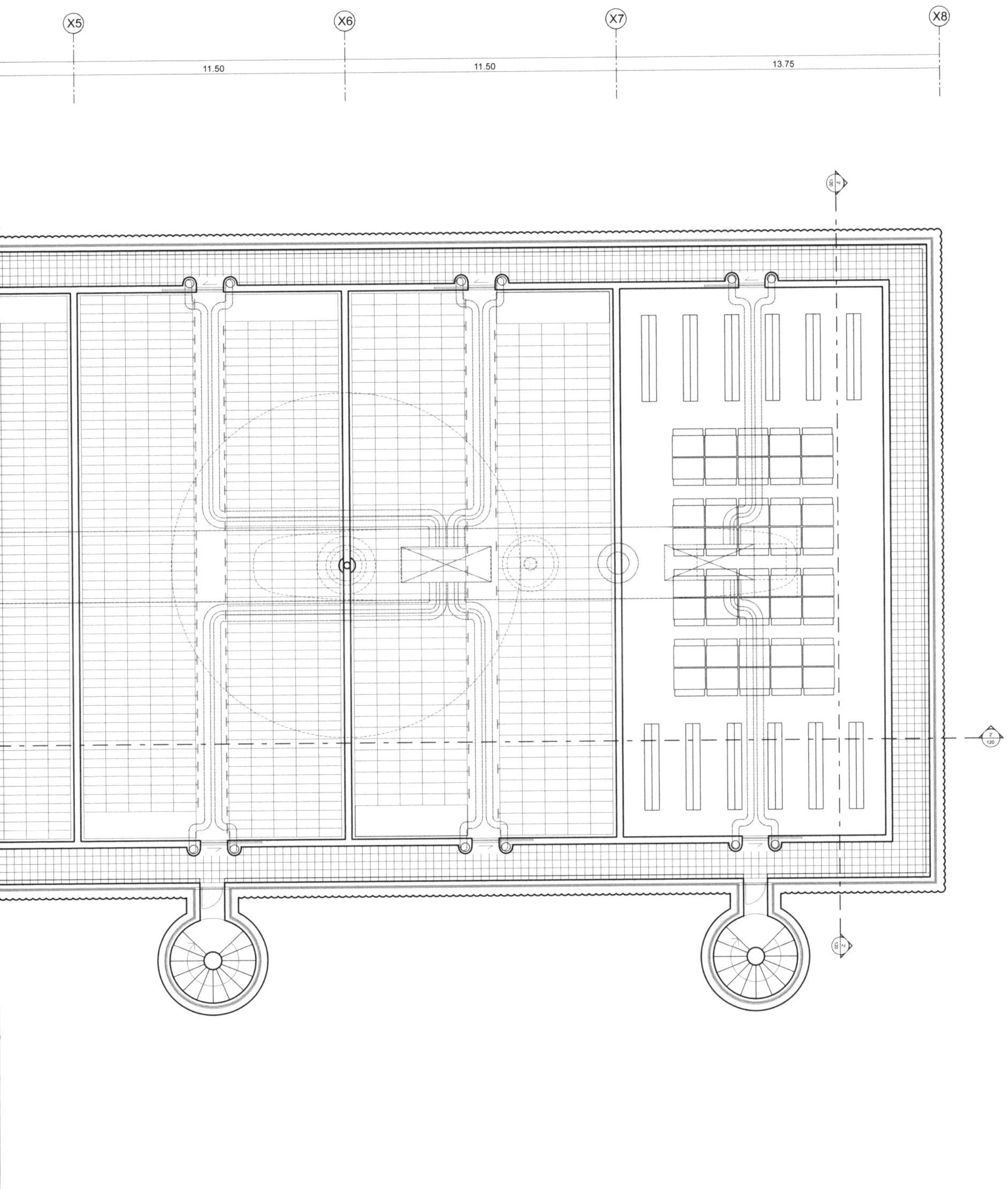
X5
X6
X7
X8
11.50
11.50
13.75
Y1
Y2
Y2
Y3
Y4
7.50

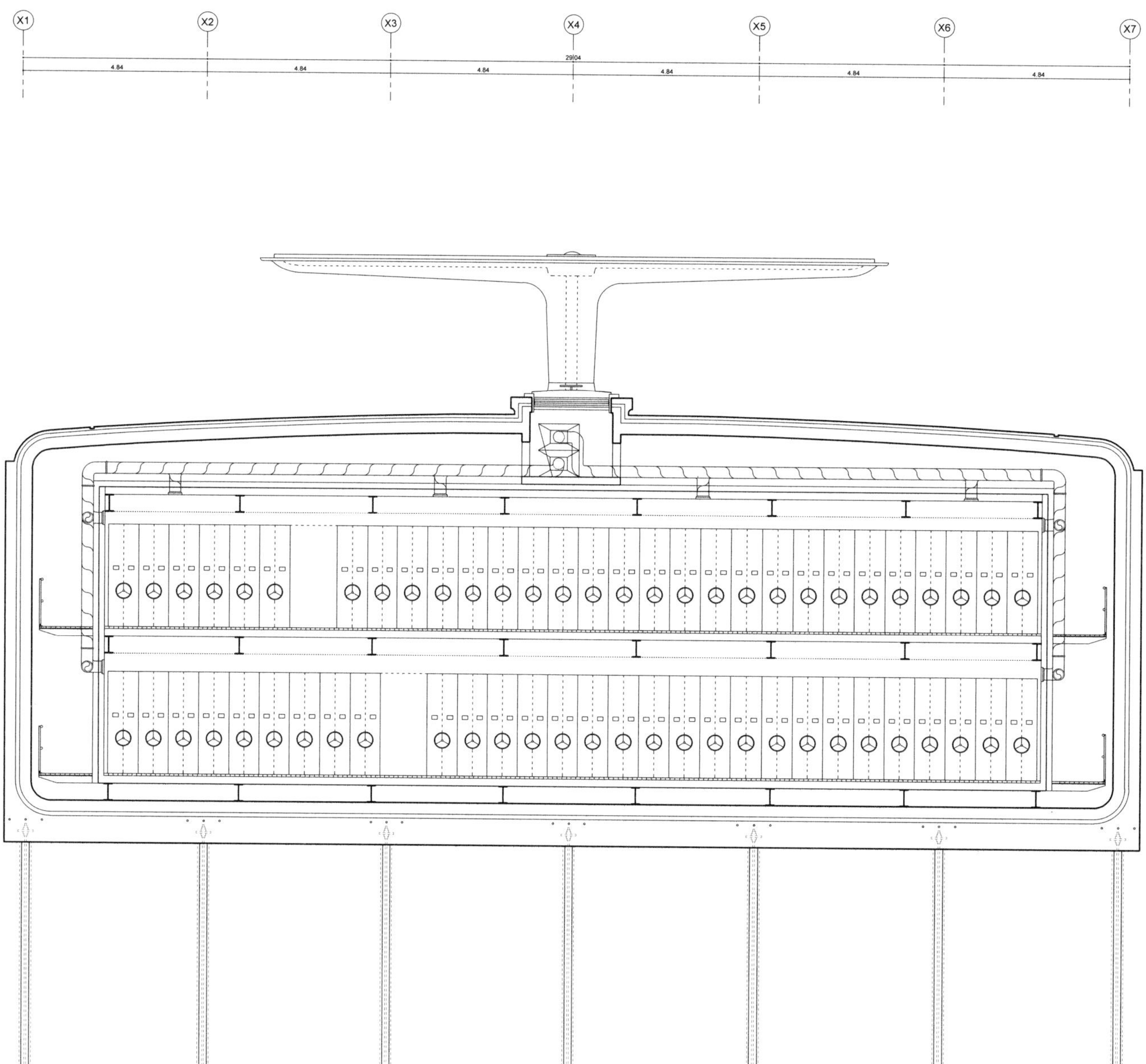

HÔTEL DES ARCHIVES, State Archives

Baukunst was founded by Adrien Verschuere in 2008 in Brussels, Belgium, and from 2017 in Lausanne, Switzerland. A conjunction of sciences and arts, the office engages the architectural medium as a dialogic tool for gathering different forms of knowledge. Baukunst operates and creates built environments through the construction of performative objects; staging real and mnemonic, living and non-living agents.

Brussels
Belgium

QUATRE-VENTS
2010 – 2014

Pocket park
and polyvalent hall
Shortlisted competition. 1st prize.

Client:
Commune
de Molenbeek-St-Jean.
Architecture:
Baukunst.
Design team:
Benoit Delpierre,
Fabian Maricq,
Adrien Verschuere.
Landscape design:
Landinzicht – Bjorn Gielen.
Structural engineer:
Util.
General contractor:
Openair.
Image:
Maxime Delvaux.

Various
places

ARSENIC
2012

Travelling theatre
Shortlisted competition. 3rd prize.

Client:
Fédération
Wallonie-Bruxelles.
Architecture:
Baukunst.
Design team:
Benoit Delpierre,
João Pauperio,
Adrien Verschuere.
Structural engineer:
Util.
Textile design:
Chevalier Masson.
Stage consultant:
Stageco.
Image:
Artefactorylab;
Olivier Campagne.

Verviers
Belgium

HÔTEL DE BIOLLEY
2014

City history
and Fine Art Museum
Shortlisted competition. 3rd prize.

Clients:
Ville de Verviers,
Institut du Patrimoine
Wallon.
Architecture:
Baukunst.
Design team:
Aidas Krutejavas,
João Pauperio,
Adrien Verschuere.
Landscape design:
Landinzicht - Bjorn Gielen.
Structural engineer:
Stabili D.
*Mechanical and energy
engineer:*
Bureau d'Études
Pierre Berger.
Textile design:
Chevalier Masson.
Cost consultant:
Bureau Bouwtechniek.
Heritage consultant:
Origin.
Image:
Artefactorylab;
Olivier Campagne.
Maxime Delvaux.

Spa
Belgium

LA FRAINEUSE
2014 – 2017

Reception
and polyvalent building
Shortlisted competition. 1st prize.

Client:
Fédération
Wallonie-Bruxelles.
Architecture:
Baukunst.
Design team:
Benoit Delpierre,
Justine Devergnies,
Samuel Jaubert de Beaujeu,
Fabian Maricq,
Adrien Verschuere.
*Cost and execution
managment:*
Bureau Bouwtechniek.
Landscape design:
Bureau Bas Smets.
*Structural and mechanical
engineer:*
Greisch.
Energy engineer:
Bureau d'Etudes Lemaire.
Textile design:
Chevalier Masson.
General contractor:
Wust.
Image:
Maxime Delvaux.
Julien Hourcade.

Ghent
Belgium

WATERSPORTBAAN
2015

Pedestrian bridge
Shortlisted competition. 3rd prize.

Client:
Stad Gent.
Architecture:
Baukunst.
Design team:
Justine Devergnies,
Kornel Lewicki,
Adrien Verschuere,
Lorenzo Vicari,
Stefano Zeni.
Landscape design:
Landinzicht - Bjorn Gielen.
Structural engineer:
Util.
Image:
Artefactorylab;
Olivier Campagne.
Maxime Delvaux.

Brussels
Belgium

RASQUINET
2015 – 2019

Public park
and polyvalent hall
Shortlisted competition. 1st prize.

Client:
Commune de Schaerbeek,
Renovas.
Architecture:
Baukunst.
Design team:
Benoit Delpierre,
Justine Devergnies,
João, Pauperio,
Maria Rebelo,
Manuela Schönenberger,
Adrien Verschuere.
Landscape design:
Fondu Landscape Architects.
Structural engineer:
Ney & Partners.
General contractor:
Openair.
Image:
Maxime Delvaux.

Paris
France

SACLAY
2016 –

Student residence
and reversible car park
Shortlisted competition. 1st prize.

Clients:
Établissement
Public d'Aménagement
Paris-Saclay,
1001 Vies Habitat.
Architecture:
Baukunst,
Bruther.
Design team:
Hilaire Baudouin,
Guillaume Bostoen,
Charles Bourely,
Stéphanie Bru,
Gauthier Demunieux,
Benoit Delpierre,
Justine Devergnies,
Bérengère Fornalczyk,
Elisa Lorenzi,
Quentin Madiot,
João Pauperio,
Maria Rebelo,
Alexandre Theriot,
Adrien Verschuere.
Structural engineer:
Batiserf.
Mechanical and energy engineer:
Inex.
Textile design:
Chevalier Masson.
Cost consultant:
BMF.
Facade consultant:
VS-A.
Acoustic engineer:
Gamba.
General contractor:
Sicra,
Rinaldi.
Image:
Artefactorylab;
Olivier Campagne.

Tongre-Notre-Dame
Belgium

LA HUNELLE
2016 –

Community
and banquet hall
Shortlisted competition. 1st prize.

Client:
Commune de Chièvres.
Architecture:
Baukunst.
Design team:
Justine Devergnies,
Kornel Lewicki,
João Pauperio,
Maria Rebelo,
Adrien Verschuere.
Structural engineer:
Util.
Technical and energy engineer:
Pluricite.
Image:
Artefactorylab;
Olivier Campagne.

Geneva
Switzerland

BASTION
2016

Enhancement of
an archaeological site
Shortlisted competition.

Client:
République et Canton
de Genève.
Architecture:
Baukunst.
Design team:
Marta Locarno,
João Pauperio,
Maria Rebelo,
Adrien Verschuere,
Manuela Schönenberger.
Landscape Design:
MG Associés.
Structural engineer:
Muttoni & Fernandez
Ingénieurs Conseils.
Climate consultant:
Transsolar.
Image:
Artefactorylab;
Olivier Campagne.
Maxime Delvaux.

Lausanne
Switzerland

SCIENCES DE LA VIE
2017 –

Microbiology and
neuroscience research and
teaching laboratories
Shortlisted competition. 1st prize.

Client:
État de Vaud.
Architecture:
Baukunst,
Bruther.
Design team:
Antoine Barjon,
Stéphanie Bru,
Fanny Christinaz,
Justine Devergnies,
Elisa Lorenzi,
João Pauperio,
Lucas Podzuweit,
Manuel Potterat,
Manuela Schönenberger,
Alexandre Theriot,
Adrien Verschuere,
Martin Wecke.
Structural engineer:
Muttoni & Fernandez
Ingénieurs Conseils.
Mechanical engineer:
Chuard Ingénieurs Vaud.
Climate and energy engineer:
Sorane.
Textile design:
Chevalier Masson.
Facade consultant:
BCS.
Acoustic engineer:
Ecoacoustic.
Fire engineer:
Igni Salutem.
Image:
Artefactorylab;
Olivier Campagne.
Maxime Delvaux.

Brussels
Belgium

FRAME
2017 –

Television studios
and co-working offices
Shortlisted competition. 1st prize.

Client:
Société d'Aménagement
Urbain.
Architecture:
Baukunst,
Bruther.
Design team:
Guillaume Bostoen,
Stéphanie Bru,
Claudio Cortese,
Nicolò De Paoli,
Baptiste Fleury,
Paul Machedon,
Maria Rebelo,
Yann Salzmann,
Alexandre Theriot,
Adrien Verschuere,
Martin Wecke.
Landscape design:
Landinzicht - Bjorn Gielen.
Structural engineer:
Bollinger+Grohmann.
*Mechanical and energy
engineer:*
Bureau d'Études
Pierre Berger.
Textile design:
Chevalier Masson.
Cost consultant:
Bureau Bouwtechniek.
Facade consultant:
VS-A.
Acoustic engineer:
Kahle Acoustics.
Fire engineer:
Delta GC.
Image:
Artefactorylab;
Olivier Campagne.
Maxime Delvaux.

Geneva
Switzerland

HEdS
2018

Healthcare institute
Shortlisted competition. 3rd prize.

Client:
République et Canton
de Genève.
Architecture:
Baukunst.
Design team:
Clémence Allègre,
Justine Devergnies,
Kornel Lewicki,
Léonie Müller,
Adrien Verschuere,
Lorenzo Vicari.
Structural engineer:
Bollinger+Grohmann.
Mechanical engineer:
SRG.
Fire engineer:
Igni Salutem.
Image:
Artefactorylab;
Olivier Campagne.

Zürich
Switzerland

FORUM UZH
2018

Teaching and
learning centre
Shortlisted competition. 3rd prize.

Client:
Kanton Zürich.
Architecture:
Baukunst,
Bruther.
Design team:
Stéphanie Bru,
Justine Devergnies,
João Pauperio,
Lucas Podzuweit,
Manuela Schönenberger,
Alexandre Theriot,
Maja Tomljenović,
Adrien Verschuere,
Martin Wecke,
David Wessel.
Landscape design:
Mosbach paysagistes.
Structural engineer:
Bollinger+Grohmann.
Mechanical and energy engineer:
Amstein+Walthert.
Facade consultant:
Lüchinger+Meyer.
Cost consultant:
Caretta+Weidmann Baumanagment.
Climate consultant:
Transsolar.
Image:
Artefactorylab;
Olivier Campagne.

Winterthur
Switzerland

ZHAW CAMPUS
2018

Physics and mechanical
engineering laboratories
Shortlisted competition. 2nd prize.

Client:
Kanton Zürich.
Architecture:
Baukunst,
Bruther.
Design team:
Stéphanie Bru,
Quentin Clémence,
Paul Machedon,
Lucas Podzuweit,
Maria Rebelo,
Alexandre Theriot,
Maja Tomljenović,
Adrien Verschuere,
Martin Wecke.
Landscape design:
Mosbach paysagistes.
Structural engineer:
Bollinger+Grohmann.
Mechanical and energy engineer:
Amstein+Walthert.
Facade consultant:
Lüchinger+Meyer.
Cost consultant:
Pfister Partner Baumanagment.
Climate consultant:
Transsolar.
Lab consultant:
Laborplanner Tonelli.
Image:
Artefactorylab;
Olivier Campagne.

Geneva
Switzerland

HÔTEL DES ARCHIVES
2018

State Archives
Shortlisted competition.

Client:
République et Canton de Genève.
Architecture:
Baukunst.
Design team:
Guillaume Bostoen,
Maria Rebelo,
Adrien Verschuere.
Landscape design:
Maurus Schifferli.
Structural engineer:
Bollinger+Grohmann.
Mechanical engineer:
SRG.
Climate consultant:
Transsolar.
Fire engineer:
Ingni Salutem.
Image:
Artefactorylab;
Olivier Campagne.
Maxime Delvaux.

Lille
France

EURALILLE
2018

Public billboard
Shortlisted competition.

Client:
SPL-Euralille.
Architecture:
Baukunst.
Design team:
Guillaume Bostoen,
Marta Locarno,
Adrien Verschuere.
Structural engineer:
Util.
Image:
Artefactorylab;
Olivier Campagne.
Maxime Delvaux.

Addis Ababa
Ethiopia

TORHAYLOCH HILL
2018

Swiss embassy
International competition.

Client:
Schweizerische
Botschaft Addis Abeba.
Architecture:
Baukunst.
Design team:
Kornel Lewicki,
Leonie Müller,
Adrien Verschuere.
Climate consultant:
Transsolar.
Image:
Artefactorylab;
Olivier Campagne.

Forest
Belgium

NMBS
2019

Power station
Shortlisted competition. 3rd prize.

Client:
Withheld.
Architecture:
Baukunst.
Design team:
Guillaume Bostoen,
Marta Locarno,
Paul Machedon,
Adrien Verschuere,
Martin Wecke.
Structural engineer:
Util.
Climate consultant:
Transsolar.
Image:
Artefactorylab;
Olivier Campagne.
Maxime Delvaux.

Brussels
Belgium

MANUFAKTURE
2019 –

Food workshops,
reversible car park
and public swimming pool
Shortlisted competition. 1st prize.

Client:
Abattoir.
Architecture:
Baukunst.
Design team:
Guillaume Bostoen,
Benoit Delpierre,
Nicolò De Paoli,
Justine Devergnies,
Kornel Lewicki,
Felix Spangenberg,
Adrien Verschuere.
Cost consultant:
Bureau Bouwtechniek.
Structural engineer:
Util.
Mechanical engineer:
TPF.
Climate consultant:
Daidalos Peutz.
Image:
Artefactorylab;
Olivier Campagne.
Maxime Delvaux.

Brussels
Belgium

ROSAS
2019

Dance and music
rehearsal studios
Shortlisted competition.

Clients:
P.A.R.T.S.,
Ictus,
Rosas.
Architecture:
Baukunst,
Philippe Vander Maren,
Richard Venlet.
Design team:
Guillaume Bostoen,
Claudio Cortese,
Caroline Gracio-Juhue,
Adrien Verschuere,
Jacopo Zani.
Landscape design:
Bureau Bas Smets.
Structural engineer:
Util.
Mechanical and energy engineer:
Bureau d'Études
Pierre Berger.
Acoustic engineer:
Kahle Acoustics.
Image:
Artefactorylab;
Olivier Campagne.
Maxime Delvaux.

This three-part conversation between Adrien Verschuere and Hans Ulrich Obrist took place successively on Thursday 18 and Monday 22 July 2019 between the Serpentine Gallery in London, on a train, and the office of Baukunst in Brussels.

HANS ULRICH OBRIST — I would like to start at the beginning. How did you come to architecture? Because architecture is a rather general profession and not disconnected from art. So how did you begin? Was there an epiphany?

ADRIEN VERSCHUERE — Not really an epiphany but I guess it began during my studies by reading Marcel Proust's *À la recherche du temps perdu.*[1] I then developed further and more profoundly the reading of Proust which became the main topic of my thesis in collaboration with Elia Zenghelis, my studio professor. The main issue for me was to discover the value of space as a mental construction. To understand the value of a place as a sign, as a physical inscription able to articulate different times, a sort of time capsule where imagination and memory are intertwined; *une machine productrice de signes*, as Gilles Deleuze says. I remember one chapter in particular, titled *Noms de pays: le nom*, where the reality of places, signified by their names, changes and is transformed through by its memory. If I remember correctly, Marcel Proust uses a metaphor that I find very beautiful: memory as a pollination of the senses.

À la recherche du temps perdu also made me aware of the strong relationship between reality and fiction, between memory and imagination, as Godard says in *Histoire(s) du cinéma*: *Si je force le souvenir, tout d'un coup, je comprends ce qui m'arrive: j'imagine, voilà, je ne me souviens plus, j'imagine.*[2].

The Art of Memory[3] by the English historian Frances Yates was also important to me at that time. Her research talks about the essential relationship between sign, space and memory, which were used as mnemonic techniques in sixteenth-century rhetoric.

In retrospect these readings probably helped me to understand possible issues I wanted to work with as an architect. Then I became more and more interested in the idea that space could be considered as an agent of time, although we usually understand it in opposite way. If space has neither past, nor present nor future as such, I believe architecture probably has the ability to confer to space a specific time. Consequently, our main material as architects would ultimately be time rather than space. Architecture would therefore support the idea of a topological time, rather than a linear time, a "space time" where different stories and histories intersect without any continuity. This led me to embrace the history of forms and ideas in our architectural practice as a perfectly recyclable material.

You founded Baukunst in Brussels in 2008. It seems Baukunst is very much about connections and collaborations, but with a strong conception and a practical solution. Can you tell us why you called it Baukunst, and what the main ideas and strategies are that make up your projects? Is there such a thing as a Baukunst manifesto?

Since *Baukunst* simply means "architecture", it was in the beginning a question of addressing the office through a very generic and anonymous name.

Baukunst is also a word that stems from a construction, a contraction of two different words – *Bau* (construction) and *Kunst* (art) – which ultimately creates a third meaning. It is built by a montage, a *rapprochement*, of two different kinds of realities. In this sense, it also addresses my strong affinities with cinema making.

Without wanting to turn the word into a manifesto, it could ultimately be understood as a metaphore of architecture, as a discipline capable of creating links between people and things that exist, and sometimes as they already exist. I think

1. Marcel Proust, *À la recherche du temps perdu*, Paris, Gallimard, 1913–1927.
2. Jean-Luc Godard, *Histoire(s) du cinéma* [1988], Paris, Gallimard [coll. Blanche], 1999, p. 173.
3. Frances A. Yates, *The Art of Memory*, London, Routledge & Kegan Paul PLC, 1966.

that the ability to reflect on the relationships between things, much more to consider things for themselves, is undoubtedly one of our main duties as architects. This perhaps goes back to a very classical notion of architecture considered as a tool of composition, or in an other way, architecture as an "art of proportions".

I am interested in your idea of public space. What for you is public space? An example could be your 2016 project "Structure and gardens", where polyvalence and reversibility of uses provide a long-lasting platform for the city. You said you wanted to create an open-air chamber in addition to actual public buildings that would be managed and animated by local associative communities. This open-air chamber is almost what Cedric Price would have called a "magnet", right? Can you tell us about this project and your idea of public and collective space?

First of all this project is important because it is our first built project.

The link you suggest with Cedric Price is interesting because this project was indeed viewed first and foremost as "a device". The aim was to use the medium of architecture, in this case a fairly simple and almost classical structure – a roof and four columns – as a tool capable of transforming a leftover space into a public space, a pocket park. In this respect, I think this project engages another essential function of architecture which is acting on the transformation of the status of things. Architecture as a tool that can engage more fundamental transformations in parallel with the physical ones.

What seems important to me in this project is that the architectural resolution here is essentially due to its ability to produce a sign. It was indeed a question of signifying the public character of a space through a precisely built intervention. The project is therefore fundamentally linked to the construction of a sign, a sign bearing a recognizable public value, and by consequence, possibly engages our collective memory.

The significance of infrastructure is of course another connection to Cedric Price. When he came up with the idea of the *Fun Palace* with theatre director Joan Littlewood, he evoked an institution that would provide infrastructure into which we could plug all kinds of functions: slow and fast lanes, intimate but also public gatherings. I'm interested in this idea of infrastructure that you evoke and how you choose and situate a certain structure as a trigger, a starting point for a stage of conditions. A project that is of particular interest to me is your sports infrastructure in Spa, Belgium, where you use the existing topography and the artefact of the castle of *La Fraineuse* to reconfigure the site through a monolithic on-site concrete structure. It is almost as if you used the "already made", the "as found" as Peter and Alison Smithson would have said, and then built upon it. This project also contains a sense of blending and contrasting with the topography. Could you tell us about the "as found" idea?

This project pursues the idea of an infrastructure's topographical inscription in the territory. An infrastructure capable of staging a series of physical and non-physical conditions. For instance, the project creates links with the various surrounding landscapes – the visible one of the place itself, as well as the more distant ones not directly visible, such as the valley bordering the site or the *grand paysage* of dense forests and neighbouring plateaus, but also, more symbolically, through the central patio, the importance given to the the specific atmosphere of the place, sometimes humid, snowy, dry or dusty.

The superposition of these discontinuous scales within one and the same building is undoubtedly one of the main issues of this project. If the inscription of the project on the topography constitutes the physical link to the territory, it seemed necessary to find an architectural element to address the other scales, the other "landscapes". That is why we proposed an abstract architectural element like a shortcut to establish a certain continuity between these different scales. The large roof plays this role, like a complementary element which responds to the project's physical inscription in its environment. There is therefore a rather literal *mise en scène* here between two important architectural themes: infrastructure and superstructure.

Your question about the "as found" refers to what I would call "shortcuts" in the conception of our projects. The use of "as found" objects enables us to literally shortcut some formal decision to better focus on some essential conditions of the project and less on its outcome. So the idea of "as found" objects would be quite similar to the construction of an instrument capable of solving a particular problem. This approach is in line with the idea of French philosopher Gilbert Simondon,[4] who places invention precisely as an element of mediation between different operators to establish a form of compatibility between them.

Architecture exhibitions are a medium in their own right. Putting on an exhibition of models is often challenging because it's almost like showing music without playing it. For a lay audience, it is difficult to understand and that is why it's so interesting. This has stimulated a creative approach to architecture exhibitions, from the Smithsons' *House of the Future* show in London in 1956 to Giancarlo De Carlo's legendary 1968 Milano Triennale. Exhibitions were seen as a space of experience. How are you going to deal with the exhibition in BOZAR? How are you going to show models and turn it into an experience?

It is indeed a complex thing to imagine an architecture exhibition, all the more when it involves our own work. If we had decided to present the projects as such through their different representations, I would feel I was taking them out of their own reality once they had been moved to the exhibition. So, we tried to avoid this type of presentation, which seemed to contradict the way we work.

We therefore decided to focus on the dialogues that the projects could have with each other or with other objects, rather than talk mainly about the projects themselves.

The exhibition once more underlines the importance we give to the organization, or what we could call the orchestration, of things. In order to set up these "conversations", we brought together different protagonists, understood in an almost theatrical sense. Almost all of the works presented in the exhibition therefore focused on the type of game they could play together.

So, we imagined projects that are like mechanisms or automatons on different scales, models performing actions in the space, sometimes playing with the condition of the space or sometimes conversing with other objects. They will be acting as "performative objects" without the need for a human point of view or action. This naturally gave rise to the exhibition title *Performance & Performativity*.

Do you mean the models will be alive?

Yes, indeed, though I would call them mechanisms rather than models, given the way we imagined them – as mobile objects, in a certain way closely linked to robotics.

This is interesting because something new has been happening in contemporary art over the past couple of years: artists have started making exhibitions as living organisms. The French artist Philippe Parreno, for example, worked with bacteria as a trigger, Pierre Huyghe with flies and AI[5] and Hito Steyerl did a future garden

4. Gilbert Simondon, *Imagination et Invention (1965–1966)*, Chatou, Éditions de la Transparence, 2008.
5. Pierre Huyghe worked with flies in the *UUmwelt* exhibition that took place in the Serpentine Gallery in London from 3 October 2018 until 10 February 2019.

with AI. And then of course with digital art – if you think of the American artist Ian Cheng – there is more and more this idea of an exhibition as a living organism, but I haven't heard of this so much in architecture yet. So, I'm curious to hear more about your vision of this idea of an exhibition as a living organism.

Beyond the question of the exhibition itself, the idea of the "living organism" is interesting because it gives us the opportunity to imagine architecture as an active device between humans and non-humans. In a broader way, to participate in a possible shift of an anthropocentric point of view, to consider differently the relationship between nature and culture, referring here to Philippe Descola's essay *Par-delà nature et culture*.[6] In this context, Bruno Latour's proposal, when he pleads for the constitution of a *Parlement des choses*,[7] seems quite interesting for us, architects, who work and act through the construction of things; things or objects that allow a form of mediation between us, humans, and non-human protagonists. Architecture as a possible form of mediation between different scales, different objects, different environments, is quite central to the conception of our projects. We want to address this position in this exhibition as a collection of objects and projects that interact with each other, and to place them in situations they were not meant necessarly to be in together.

One of the first things that I saw of yours were the *Urban Portraits*[8] you showed in the *3 Cities* exhibition, a kind of montage that sidesteps in a sense the preciousness of an architecture proposal. They conjure the notion of utopia or what you call ideality, maybe also some kind of thinking, in Bruno Latour's meaning of the exhibition as a thought process. Can you tell us about the use of the notion of "portrait" in relation to cities? It is very difficult to portray a city because it can change all of a sudden. So, it is difficult to find a synthetic image of the city, and it is a near impossibility to make a portrait of a city in that sense. I'm interested in what these *Urban Portraits* are and whether it is at all possible to make a portrait of a city.

The *Urban Portraits* initiative grew out of the desire to engage the medium of the image as a tool to help us think about the projects, to think with the image rather than outside of it. Instead of building image as an illustration of a given project, which necessarily induces an almost unilateral point of view, we wanted to engage the possibility of the image as an open form. We wanted to move our attention, consider urban issues through a very literal reading of its morphology, rather than addressing the architectural object for itself. And then it was also an experimentation about the construction of images by the use of different technologies, among other aerial views shoted from helicopter. We wanted indeed to experiment if we could achieve a kind of intensity by means of precise technologies, and ultimately with hyper-realistic images.

It is probably no coincidence that, at the time, I was both immersed in the neorealism found in the early works of Roberto Rossellini and Michelangelo Antonioni and, at the same time, interested in the idea of "speculative fiction" put forward by the American philosopher Donna Haraway. These works seemed particularly stimulating to me because they advocated generic ambiguity, and a very fine nuance between documentary and fiction; one could say between actual and virtual.

6. Philippe Descola, *Par-delà nature et culture* [2005], Paris, Gallimard [coll. Folio essais], 2015.
7. Bruno Latour, *Nous n'avons jamais été modernes. Essai d'anthropologie symétrique,* Paris, La Découverte, 1991.
8. The urban portraits are three monumental photographic montages that present a critical approach of the cities of Liège, Bruges and Brussels.

This ties in with your question on the portrait. Mirroring our activity in the office, where projects are built by iteration between analysis and speculation, we wanted to use the pretext of this research to place the speculative part of the project much closer to the descriptive part.

The idea was to produce these images according to very precise rules but not necessarily based on the reality of a proposal as such. It was a matter of situating the action of the project, in a rather paradoxical way, by erasing or substituting fragments of certain urban contexts rather than by adding new elements as we are used to doing in our everyday practice.

Ultimately, we also wanted to test the narrative capacity of these images, the possibility of diverse interpretations, among the widest possible audience. We therefore, decided to show this research in our first solo exhibition, *3 Cities*, which took place in the Centre for Fine Arts in Brussels in 2009.

I also wanted to ask you about utopia, because I've always been interested in this notion, in Yona Friedman's sense of the *utopie concrète*. It's interesting that you reject the traditional understanding of utopia as a conception of "no place" exemplified by Sir Thomas More in his socio-political satire of 1516. You have actually used Friedman's term "concrete utopia" to denote a certain position of resistance based on a desire to continue building real things. Can you tell us a bit about your criticism of the Morian utopia and what you mean by "concrete utopia"?

The use of Yona Friedman's word *réalisable* seems to follow the idea of utopia as a concept very close to reality which I totally follow. Indeed, I am little interested in the idea of utopia as an illusion of a better world, imagined outside the world itself, as an extraction of reality.

I prefer to rethink things from within, on the basis of the very existence of things, to try to offer new articulations or new perspectives in order to build ultimately new intensities. This is probably what we are seeking, through the objects we produce, a certain intensity addressing itself to different times and spaces from the current state of the project. We are looking, I think, for something that goes beyond the contingencies strictly related to their use or their construction, we could say that we look for another kind of "presence".

Another relevant notion is resistance. An experiment in the format of an exhibition was of course Jean-François Lyotard's *Les Immatériaux* in the early days of the Pompidou Centre. This exhibition was ahead of its time because it really looked into information, technology and cybernetics. It was meant to be followed by a second exhibition that Lyotard wanted to curate and entitle *Résistance*, not only in the sense of political resistance, but also of physical and scientific resistances. Philippe Parreno, Daniel Birnbaum and I are planning to realize this unrealized show within The Luma Foundation. Lyotard wanted the second exhibition to be a film, because he saw the exhibition as a difficult medium since it has a limited lifespan and is difficult to document. I would like to ask you about the resistance in your work.

Resistance is indeed a central theme in our practice because it naturally involves a whole series of moral and possibly political issues, but also, in our case, a very concrete dimension. We could talk of the *Résistance des (im)matériaux* to play with the starting point of your question.

In our work, resistance evokes quite literally the question of structure. The structural issue is often central in our work. Beyond its bearing capacity, I guess it enables us to focus on the organization of and experimentation with the various conditions of the project early on in its formalization.

And then, in a more general way, the structure indirectly raises the question of our relationship to gravity, which we could in fact understand as a common value, a kind of "common good", potentially connecting us to all other terrestrial elements.

I'm always interested in the unrealized projects of artists and architects. One particular project that has fascinated me greatly is the travelling theatre you made for a competition. It relates to your exhibition because it has to do with staging and utility, and the functionality and idiosyncrasy of how it is used and activated. When I asked Louise Bourgeois what her unrealized projects were, she also talked about her project for an amphitheatre. Yours would actually be mobile. Can you tell us a little bit more about your mobile theatre?

I guess our proposal for a travelling theatre addresses another issue I find important: that of theatricality in architecture.

Since we work on changing the status of things, theatricality is quite fundamental in our practice. When you consider architecture as a device, one of its essential functions lies in its ability to stage people and things, and from this perspective it confers to architecture a performative capacity. Working on the design of a theatre therefore raises the very question of theatricality.

If, for this type of programme, architecture often strives to extract the action from its context, we wanted to do the opposite for this project, i.e. be able to integrate the action into its context as much as possible to reinforce the ambiguity between different realities. The theatre therefore develops in complete continuity with the public space and, depending on the performances, is set up in very different environments.

The theatre is both present as a stable form, but also absent by the instability of the places in which it settles. In a sense, it is therefore not only a highly architectural, referenced, functional and efficient object, but also in a certain way non-architectural because of its totally abstract and deterritorialized character.

The artist Martha Rosler said that the future always flies in under the radar. I want to finish by asking you about the future. What's going to happen with Baukunst in the near and distant future? What are your main objectives for the next ten years?

If I remember correctly, there is an aphorism of Paul Valéry in one of his *Cahiers*, which says that it would be beautiful to be able to think in a form that does not yet exist. Even if this may at first seem unthinkable, it nevertheless seems to me a rather exciting prospect for work!

More specifically, I would like to maintain the intensity with which we are currently doing things. I would like to continue to consider projects essentially as research tools, to continue to approach the projects as means of open conversation with the world around us.

Among the things surrounding us, one of the possible conversations would be to engage architecture as "an environment", potentially capable of addressing other life forms. Jakob von Uexküll's theory of the *Umwelt*,[9] which seems to have been one influence of your past exhibition with Pierre Huyghe, would be particularly interesting to engage with in this regard.

That is a great way of commemorating Michel Serres, who just passed away. Was he important to you also?

Michel Serres is indeed someone I have been reading regularly for a long time. What I probably appreciate most about him is his ability to set thoughts in motion. Just like the way he writes. I have always been fascinated by his agility in linking things in a logical and yet totally unexpected way. Most of his writings also touch me because they produce perfectly hybrid objects, one could say located between

9. Jakob von Uexküll, *A Foray into the Worlds of Animals and Humans: with A Theory of Meaning* [1934], Minneapolis, University of Minnesota Press, 2010.

poèmes and *théorèmes*. There are also many discoveries in his proposals, such as the notion of *quasi-objets* that offers the possibility to open the way we see and potentially transform things.

Rainer Maria Rilke wrote a little book consisting of advice to young poets. And, as you know, this is another recurring question in my interviews. It is somewhat paradoxical, since you are still a young architect, but what is your advice to a young architect in 2019?

The question of mobility seems to me to be fundamental. I think my main piece of advice is "be mobile".

This brings us back to the mobile theatre, to the start of the interview. How can an architect be mobile? Because obviously architecture is often also connected to an office. Ralf Erskin, Swedish architect and member of Team X, moved his office to a boat in the Swedish archipelago because he said architects have to be mobile. But maybe this isn't what you mean. Can you tell us more?

I understand mobility as both the precise definition of a specific position and the possibility of considering others. Ideally, this should happen simultaneously!

Mobility also leads us to imagine a project as one probability among many others instead of a definitive answer as such. Making a project would therefore be both to propose fairly precise choices according to certain parameters, and to keep a very open and porous look on their potential of interaction or interpretation. The beauty of doing projects would therefore relies on paradoxical positions, we could say between mastering and displaying. The film *Zidane: A 21st Century Portrait*[10] would be a good metaphor to illustrate this attitude. What particularly touches me in this work is the player's extreme obsession and precision but also, at the same time, his extreme availability, almost like a form of improvisation as the game unfolds. I find this attitude particularly evocative of how I view the way we try to work.

10. Movie by Douglas Gordon and Philippe Parreno, distributed by Universal Studios, 2006.

This interview is dedicated to the memory of Michel Serres.

PUBLICATION

Editors:
Roxane Le Grelle,
Iwan Strauven,
Adrien Verschuere.
In collaboration with
Lara Molino.
Authors:
Lynn Margulis
and Dorion Sagan,
Jacques Lafitte,
Adrien Verschuere
in conversation with
Hans Ulrich Obrist.
Graphic Design:
Atelier Olivier Lamy
with Olivier Bertrand.
Font:
Immortel
by Clément Le Tulle-Neyret.
Photography:
ArtefactoryLab;
Olivier Campagne
with Hadrien Hartgers,
Adeline Habert,
Guillaume Roger.
Maxime Delvaux.
Julien Hourcade.
Graphic documents:
Baukunst;
Adrien Verschuere
with Marta Locarno,
Lorenzo Vicari.
Orthophotography:
ArtefactoryLab;
Olivier Campagne
with Hadrien Hartgers,
Adeline Habert,
Guillaume Roger.
In collaboration with
Atlas of Place;
Thomas Paturet.
Lithography:
Mistral;
Olivier Dengis.
Translation:
Patrick Lennon.
Proofreading
& Copyediting:
Mathieu Lomax.
Publisher:
Koenig Books, London;
A+ Architecture in
Belgium, Brussels;
BOZAR Books,
Brussels.
Print:
Cassochrome.
Support:
Fédération
Wallonie Bruxelles,
Vlaamse Overheid,
Niko.

EXHIBITION

Director of exhibitions:
Sophie Lauwers.
Architecture programme:
Iwan Strauven.
Curators:
Roxane Le Grelle,
Iwan Strauven,
Adrien Verschuere.
In collaboration with
Lara Molino,
Lorenzo Vicari.
Head of production:
Evelyne Hinque.
Exhibition design:
Baukunst.
Technical coordination:
Frederic Oulieux,
Colin Fincoeur.
Models and robotics:
Julien Dutertre
and Loop Studio.
In collaboration with
Antoine Rocca,
Baukunst;
Guillaume Bostoen,
Lorenzo Vicari.
Photography:
ArtefactoryLab;
Olivier Campagne.
Maxime Delvaux.
Julien Hourcade.
Film:
ArtefactoryLab;
Olivier Campagne.
Maxime Delvaux.
Translations:
Michael Lomax.
Nathalie Tabury.
Proofreading
& Copyediting:
Copytaaldelete,
Benoit Frances,
Mathieu Lomax.
Print:
TAVU.
With the dedicated
support of:
Axelle Ancion,
Serge Blondeel,
Olivier Boruchowitch,
Francelle Cane,
Francis Carpentier,
Leen Daems,
Amina Dahman,
Justine Detienne,
Emma Dumartheray,
Koenraad Impens,
Barbara Porteman,
Olivier Rouxhet,
Guilliana Venlet,
Sylvie Verbeke,
the BOZAR art handlers
and our hosts.
Support:
Fédération
Wallonie-Bruxelles,
Vlaamse Overheid,
AR-CO insurance
cooperative for designers
in the building sector,
Bureau Bouwtechniek,
Delta Light,
Knauf,
Kone,
Legrand/BTicino,
MicomDoor,
Modena/Archicad,
Niko,
Pianos Maene,
SchermNed.
Special thanks to:
Olivier Campagne,
Maxime Delvaux,
Julien Dutertre,
Gaël Kervoas,
Nawri Khamallah,
Hans Ulrich Obrist,
Gwennaëlle Libert,
Sonia Levy,
Julien Maire,
Dorion Sagan,
Erwin Viray,
all current and former
collaborators of
Baukunst.

FÉDÉRATION WALLONIE-BRUXELLES
Vlaanderen verbeelding werkt
niko Illuminating ideas.

CENTRE FOR FINE ARTS, BRUSSELS (BOZAR)

CEO – Artistic Director:
Paul Dujardin.
Financial Director:
Jérémie Leroy.
Operations Director:
Albert Wastiaux.
Exhibitions Director:
Sophie Lauwers.
Music Director:
Ulrich Hauschild.
Human Resources Director:
Ignace De Breuck.
Secretary General:
Didier Verboomen.
Head of Cinema:
Juliette Duret.
Head of Artistic Policy Development:
Anna Vondracek.
Head of Marketing & Communication:
Sandrine Demolin.
Commercial Manager:
Luc Préaux.
ICT Manager:
François Pettiaux.
Investments, Security & Archives Manager:
Stéphane Vanreppelen.
Facility Manager:
Guillaume Creusat.
Logistics Manager:
Rudi Anneessens.
Audience Engagement Manager:
Tine Van Goethem.
Public Services Manager:
Matthieu Vanderdonckt.
Box Office Manager:
Chantal Matthys.
Planning Manager:
Cédric Orban.

A+
ARCHITECTURE IN BELGIUM

President:
Philémon Wachtelaer.
Artistic Director:
Lisa De Visscher.
Business Director:
Steven Palmaers.
Programme Coordinators:
Roxane Le Grelle,
Lara Molino.
Funding and advertising:
Rita Minissi.
Communication:
Louise Van Laethem.
Adjunct editor in chief:
Eline Dehullu.
Production Coordinator:
Grégoire Maus.
Office Manager:
Deborah Schwarzbaum.

BAUKUNST
Founded in 2008 by Adrien Verschuere.

Present collaborators:
Guillaume Bostoen,
Claudio Cortese,
Pauline Clarot,
Benoît Delpierre,
Nicolò De Paoli,
Justine Devergnies,
Tomas Devos,
Bérengère Fornalczyk,
Kornel Lewicki,
Bianca Schifani,
Sofia Sinem,
Lorenzo Vicari.
Past collaborators:
Clémence Allegre,
Anna Bazzo,
Romain Bihr,
Sofia Boldrini,
Vincenzo Bonarrigo,
Charles Bourely,
Federico Broggini,
Mauro Calderone,
Francelle Cane,
Gianmarco Causi,
Lodovico Corsini,
Florence Detienne,
Catia Esteves,
Caroline Gracio-Juhue,
Samuel Jaubert de Beaujeu,
Aïdas Krutejavas,
Julien Lapeyronie,
Marta Locarno,
Elisa Lorenzi,
Paul Machedon,
Fabian Maricq,
Leonie Müller,
João Paupério,
Lucas Podzuweit,
Maria Rebelo,
Inês Reis,
Clément Ringot,
Yann Salzmann,
Manuela Schönenberger,
Felix Spangenberg,
André Tajchman,
Maja Tomljenović,
Nelson Van Campenhout,
Martin Wecke,
Jacopo Zani,
Stefano Zeni.

Rue des Alliés –
Bondgenotenstraat, 68
1190 Brussels, Belgium

Rue du Maupas 28
1004 Lausanne,
Switzerland

© 2019 BAUKUNST, A+, BOZAR, the authors and KOENIG BOOKS, London.

All rights reserved. No part of this publication may be reproduced, stored in a computerized databank, or published or transmitted in any form or by any means, electronic or mechanical, including photocopy, recording or any other information storage or retrieval system, without prior permission in writing from the publisher. Each author is responsible for the content of their article.

FIRST PUBLISHED BY KOENIG BOOKS, LONDON
Koenig Books Ltd
At the Serpentine Gallery
Kensington Gardens
London W2 3XA
www.koenigbooks.co.uk

Printed in Belgium.

DISTRIBUTION

Germany, Austria, Switzerland/Europe:
Buchhandlung
Walther König
Ehrenstr. 4,
D-50672 Köln
Tel: +49 (0) 221 / 20 59 6 53
verlag@buchhandlung-walther-koenig.de
UK & Ireland:
Cornerhouse Publications
Ltd. – HOME
2 Tony Wilson Place,
UK – Manchester M15 4FN
Tel: +44 (0) 161 212 3466
publications@cornerhouse.org
Outside Europe:
D.A.P. / Distributed Art Publishers, Inc.
75 Broad Street, Suite 630,
USA – New York, NY 10004
Tel: +1 (0) 212 627 1999
orders@dapinc.com

ISBN 978-3-96098-683-6